DECORATING
IDEAS THAT WORK

DECORATING
IDEAS THAT WORK
Creative design solutions for your home

HEATHER J. PAPER

The Taunton Press

The Taunton Press
Inspiration for hands-on living®

The Taunton Press, Inc.,
63 South Main Street, PO Box 5506,
Newtown, CT 06470-5506
e-mail: tp@taunton.com

Editor: Jennifer Matlack
Interior design: Carol Petro
Layout: David Giammattei
Illustrator: Christine Erikson
Front cover photos: (top row, left to right) © Tria Giovan; © Eric Roth; © Eric Roth;
(bottom, clockwise from left) © Tria Giovan; © Mark Lohman; © Eric Roth;
© davidduncanlivingston.com
Front flap photo: © Tria Giovan
Back cover photos: (clockwise from top left) © Tria Giovan; © Eric Roth; © Eric Roth;
© Tria Giovan; © Ken Gutmaker; © Eric Roth
Back flap photos: (clockwise from top left) © Tim Street-Porter; © Eric Roth;
© Brian Vanden Brink; © Eric Roth

Library of Congress Cataloging-in-Publication Data
Paper, Heather J.
  Decorating ideas that work / Heather J. Paper.
      p. cm.
  Includes index.
  ISBN 978-1-56158-950-0
  1. Interior decoration. I. Title.

NK2115.P279 2007
747--dc22

                                           2007003177

Printed in the United States of America
10 9 8 7 6 5 4 3 2

The following manufacturers/names appearing in *Decorating Ideas That Work* are trademarks:
Pez®, Velcro®, Wedgewood®

ACKNOWLEDGMENTS

I was lucky enough to work with The Taunton Press a few years ago when they asked me to write the *Decorating Idea Book*. That journey proved to be a thrill ride, so I jumped at the chance when invited to author this book, too. Motivating me every day was my editor, Carolyn Mandarano, whose support, advice, and thoughtful queries inspired me to produce my very best. Every writer should be so lucky as to work with such a consummate pro. My thanks, too, go to Niki Palmer, who had the unenviable task of keeping track of every single photograph, and Jenny Peters, who kept me organized.

The words throughout this book would mean far less without the accompanying imagery; I'm indebted to all of the photographers who shared their work—and their time—so willingly. A special thank you goes to Eric Roth and his studio manager, Sabrina Velandry, as well as Mark Lohman. Whenever I needed a photograph to illustrate a certain point, they came back with not just one option but multiple choices.

Undertaking a project of this kind wouldn't be possible without the support of family and friends. Thank you, Mom, for passing along some of your incredible artistic talent; I'm convinced that's largely responsible for my choosing to make a career of interior design. And thanks to you, Dad, for your encouragement every step of the way. During the course of this project, too, friends were more supportive than I could have ever hoped, understanding when I couldn't just drop everything at a moment's notice. A special thank you, though, goes to Rick Baye, whose design talent I admire and friendship I cherish. My deep gratitude also goes to Clinton Smith; he continues to inspire me to view and think about design in fresh new ways.

A very special thank you goes to my "personal assistants." Murphy and Dickens, my two shih tzus, were with me in the office every day; just looking at them makes me smile and, sometimes, that's all the attitude adjustment I needed to clear the next hurdle. Most of all, though, I'm deeply grateful to my husband, Russ. There wasn't a day that went by that he didn't ask what he could do to help so that I could devote as much time as I needed to the book. Thank you, endlessly, for your love and your encouragement.

CONTENTS

INTRODUCTION

The importance of "home" can be credited to one thing: family. More than a touch point between activities, today's home is a safe haven, a place to relax, unwind, and reconnect. Because people are opting to spend more time at home, they want their surroundings to be comfortable—not just from a physical point of view but from a visual one as well. The full-time mom may be most interested in a homey kitchen while an executive-type might want the ultimate master suite, one where he or she can truly escape the pressures of the day. A well-outfitted home office invariably appeals to a telecommuter, while someone who entertains frequently will put more emphasis on the living and dining rooms.

The good news is that there are as many decorating possibilities as there are points of view. It's simply a matter of determining your priorities and personal preferences, then translating them to a room scheme. Creating comfortable living quarters, however, is more than a matter of shopping for a new piece of furniture from time to time; it means starting with a master plan—one that takes into account the wants and needs of every family member. (Yes, that includes the dog, too, if the family pet lives indoors and is allowed on the furniture.) And there are more resources than ever to help you carry out your design strategy. If you prefer to use a professional interior designer, he or she will have access to countless to-the-trade-only furnishings. On the other hand, the do-it-yourselfer doesn't have to give up a thing in terms of style; from furniture stores and boutiques to a virtual wealth of online resources, good design is readily accessible. Simply put, creativity doesn't have a price tag, as you'll find while you page through this book.

Here, you'll find luxurious spaces as well as those decorated on a dime. You'll find spacious lofts and diminutive dining rooms, colorful kids' rooms and subdued master suites. In short, you'll find inspiration for every style and every decorating budget. All the options are here—including the pros and cons of decorative elements—and then it's up to you. Just keep in mind that decorating is an evolution, a never-ending process. But as long as you follow your heart, your home will suit *you*. And nothing else really matters.

DESIGNING

Your dream home—one that is functional and fashionable,

just as comfortable as it is comforting—is within reach.

YOUR HOME

The best part: It doesn't take much more than some careful planning.

Start with the Big Picture

Whether you're planning a major decorating project or simply freshening up a bit, the first step in any successful redo is a little self-introspection. The needs of a young family, for instance, are completely different from those of empty nesters. Likewise, people more comfortable in a casual surround will approach things differently from those who prefer more formality. So start by asking yourself a few questions. Who will use the room and how? Is it a space that's utilized on a daily basis or one that only sees occasional use?

Part of the process, too, is to consider what architectural assets your room offers. A living room with a grand fireplace, for example, has its own "built-in" focal point. In a space that's nothing more than a square box, however, you'll need to bring in a center of focus such as a stately armoire or an eye-catching work of art.

What pieces do you own that will work into the new scheme and which additional ones will you need to purchase? Are there any physical restrictions for the furnishings on your wish list? A grand piano might be lovely but not if it won't fit through the door (or window). And a majestic cupboard may be just the thing to accommodate all of your dinnerware, but it's hardly suitable if it's too tall for your room.

Because budget is a big part of the equation, it's also important to prioritize. Don't feel that you have to complete everything on your wish list at once; some of the best-dressed rooms evolve over time, adapting to the ever-changing needs of you and your family along the way.

top and bottom • Leather sofas and chairs are some of the most comfortable, and durable, seating pieces you'll find. Their inherent dark colors, though, need to be balanced with lighter items, like the pine storage pieces and sisal rug in this room.

Put It on Paper

If you're working on a new room arrangement, resist the temptation to start pushing your furniture around. Put your plans on paper first. Start with a piece of ¼-in. grid paper, then measure your room carefully and sketch it onto the grid, including features such as windows and doors, electrical outlets, and architectural elements. Next, measure the furniture that you plan to use, and make ¼-in. templates that represent them. Make several copies then cut them out, moving them around on your floor plan until you find a look you like. If you'd rather, you can purchase room-planning kits or find the tools you need on select Internet sites.

ONE ROOM TWO WAYS

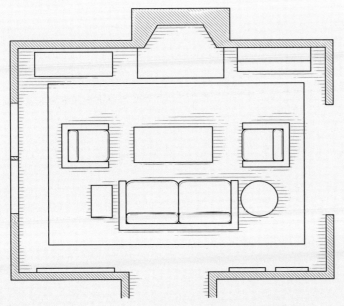

- A symmetrical arrangement creates a formal feeling.
- A fireplace serves as a natural focal point.
- A media cabinet on one side of the fireplace visually balances storage on the other.
- End tables in different shapes keep the room from feeling rigid.

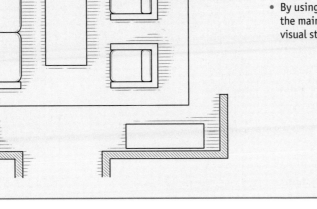

- A sofa is visually balanced by a pair of chairs, creating a more informal feeling.
- By placing the sofa at a right angle to the fireplace wall, your eye is led across the room, visually squaring up the space.
- By using two chairs, instead of one long sofa, on the main "entry" side of the room, there's less of a visual stopping point.

Once you have a clear view of your "ultimate" room, including a list of the major pieces of furniture you'll need, you can concentrate on other elements. Using the patterns and colors in your upholstered pieces as inspiration, select wall coverings that provide a complementary setting. If there's plenty of pattern in your upholstery, you may want a wall covering on the quiet side. On the other hand, solid-color sofas and chairs can be a great counterpoint for something livelier.

Next, consider window treatments: Are you looking for lush, floor-length draperies or something more tailored, such as Roman shades? Practicality may come into play, whether it's privacy needs in the bedroom and bath or room-darkening requirements for someone who works the night shift. Then, focus on the floor. This large expanse of space can greatly influence the look of your décor, and you might be surprised by the vast number of options available today. Last but not least, the right lighting will make your entire scheme shine, just as carefully selected accessories will reflect your personality.

Once you're ready to start shopping, assemble a notebook that includes your wish list as well as room dimensions and furniture measurements. Your notebook should have pockets, too, where you can stash paint chips, wallpaper samples, and fabric swatches—anything that will help take the guesswork out of the process. Have your notebook with you at all times, you never know when you might stumble across that perfect piece. And don't leave home without a steel measuring tape!

top · Give guests a clue to your personal style from the moment they step through the front door. This entry—with its simply designed chest and unpretentious accessories—leaves no doubt that country style prevails throughout this house.

bottom · A pair of sofas arranged at right angles or an L-shaped sectional can visually divide living and dining spaces in one large room. This example adheres to the same concept but uses a backless bench instead, so the eye pauses at the "dividing line" briefly but isn't completely stopped.

above • Symmetrical design can be extremely formal, but it's more lighthearted here thanks to the combined traditional and contemporary furnishings. A pair of armless chairs and an ottoman show off their leggy bases, creating a more open and airy look in the process.

Selecting a Style

Let's say you have a clear idea of your personal style. Perhaps it's truly traditional, reminiscent of Grandmother's house. Or maybe you're more of an urbanist, one who opts for sleek contemporary settings.

But if you're not sure what *your* style is, don't despair. And don't feel alone. With the wealth of home furnishings available today, it can be confusing—even intimidating—to wade through all the options. A simple exercise, though, can give you some insight. Thumb through decorating magazines, looking for rooms that you find appealing; even if some aren't the same kind of space that you're working on, there will be some elements that will translate to your room. Don't limit yourself to overall looks that you like; search for individual ideas (a storage solution or the perfect floor plan) and elements (a stunning wall covering or the ideal sofa). You may even find that you want to add some of those elements to your personal wish list. (Be sure to check the magazine's resource section for where to buy a particular piece that you like.)

Maybe you're a traditionalist. Or you prefer country style. You may even opt for contemporary quarters, whether your home has similar architecture or not. Don't be surprised, either, if you find that you like elements of several different styles, putting you in the "eclectic" category. Surround a traditional dining table with contemporary metal chairs; as long as the contrasting styles have clean, classic forms, they'll work together wonderfully. Above all, keep in mind that there are no right or wrong decorating decisions. There are guidelines, to be sure, but the bottom line is that it's all a matter of personal style—yours.

above • A country-style pencil-post bed takes center stage here, complete with top railings that can accommodate bed curtains at some future point. Painted a deep blue, the sleeping spot is sculptural in its own right.

Working with an Interior Designer

Using an interior designer can be a good investment; not only can these professionals save you time, but they can save you money, too. They know precisely where to go to find the right furnishings and can offer advice on where you can save and where you should splurge. And they can often find creative new ways to incorporate pieces you already have. The right designer for you is someone with whom you can be completely honest—and vice versa. You should be able to talk openly about what you do and don't like and what you can and can't afford. These pros also have access to many furniture lines that you won't find in retail stores; these "to-the-trade" pieces can only be purchased through interior designers.

Some designers charge a flat fee for a project, while others bill by the hour. Or they may charge a percentage of materials and labor or even go by "cost plus," where you'll pay retail costs for your furnishings and the designer's fee is the difference between that price and what he or she paid wholesale.

left · A mirrored surface covers the wall over this sink, completely visible where you need it most for grooming purposes but enhanced, architecturally, on either side. The result is a decorative element that seemingly doubles the entire space.

below · The furnishings throughout this living room speak directly to traditional style. Because the French doors and accompanying transoms are void of heavy window treatments, however, the space has an updated ambience.

STEEPED IN TRADITION

Traditional interiors are primarily based on furniture styles—both American and British—that date back to the late 18th and early 19th centuries. While some of those treasured antiques can still be found, the look remains readily accessible through any number of reproductions (line-for-line copies of the original designs) and adaptations (slightly altered in size and/or design to better suit today's lifestyles). Additionally, many pieces with French and Scandinavian pedigrees fit into this category, as well as those from other European countries. They're often referred to as "period" styles, including Georgian and Colonial, Federal and Regency, Queen Anne and Victorian, Louis XV and Louis XVI, as well as the German-based Biedermeier.

Not surprisingly, today's traditional style is interpreted in a wide variety of ways. A camelback sofa, for instance, might be covered in pure white linen to give it a fresh look. Likewise, a swag-and-jabot window treatment might be fabricated from an ethereal gauze instead of a more expected damask or silk. And therein lies the real beauty—you can give traditional style your own twist.

right · When planning a dining room, traditional or otherwise, allow plenty of space for a diner to pull back a chair and for people to pass behind him. The generous amount of "breathing room" here enhances the dining room's elegant ambience.

facing page top · Classic furniture forms wrapped with fresh fabrics create an updated traditional look. The yellows and greens in this living room were inspired by the primitive artwork on the mantel, all anchored by a plaid rug that pulls everything together.

ELEMENTS OF STYLE

Traditional

- Camelback, Empire, or chesterfield sofas
- Chippendale, Queen Anne, Sheraton, and Hepplewhite chairs
- Dark woods, most often cherry or mahogany
- Tables with turned or cabriole legs
- Velvet, silk, damask, and jacquard fabrics
- Dressmaker details on upholstered pieces, such as kick pleats, button tufting, and bullion fringe
- Elaborate window treatments with swags and jabots
- Needlepoint, Aubusson, and Oriental rugs

above • Simple elegance best describes this living/dining area, where light and dark neutrals play off one another to define furnishings and architectural elements. The rail and banisters of the stairway echo the wood tone of the dining table, leading your eye from the eating area right on up to the second floor.

Up-to-Date Traditional Style

There's perhaps no more traditional a color scheme than blue and white. In this great room, though, that classic twosome takes a fresh approach. A subtly striped wall covering, in a creamy white, provides a clean canvas for the room. From there, assorted shades of blue anchor the conversation grouping—the solid hue of the sofa, the floral-patterned chairs, and even the area rug. No two are precisely the same shade, but that only makes the room more interesting. Because they have similar tones and intensities, the colors blend together beautifully. (If you're wondering about your own group of hues, try this simple test: Gather them together, then step back. If, when you look at them through partially squinted eyes, they appear to become a single shade, you've got a good blend.)

In the adjacent dining area, the blue-and-white theme reappears in the form of another pattern, a floral stripe light enough that it doesn't detract from the view out the bay window. The shapely valance translates to the kitchen as well, where it serves as a topper for a pair of windows and conceals a privacy shade.

The room's predominant blue hue isn't restricted to soft surfaces, either. It also shows up in rect-angular tiles and granite, used both for counter-tops and a backsplash behind the commercial cooktop. These large masses of color, in fact, are what give the room its balance; they provide equilibrium for the upholstered seating pieces by the fireplace.

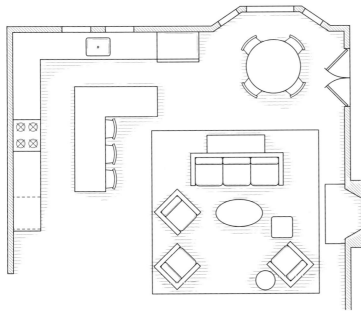

above · Raised-panel cabinetry in the kitchen continues the great room's traditional style. Even the counter stools have their own sense of history; the X-shaped backs date to Grecian times.

facing page top · Even the most traditional furnishings can get an up-to-date look with contemporary fabrics. These fabrics have modern-day appeal, even though they're applied to classic forms.

facing page bottom · The ceiling of this entire space is painted a pale shade of blue, inconspicuously lowering it from a visual point of view and cozying up the great room in the process.

CASUAL COUNTRY

A casual version of traditional style, country décor has an inherent rustic charm. It's a warm and unpretentious look that's right in line with today's laid-back lifestyles. The first mention of "country style" typically conjures up images of distressed wooden furniture with wrought iron hardware. And, in fact, that American Country interpretation remains very popular today.

There are, however, a number of other translations of country style:

• **English Country.** This style is characterized by slipcovered furniture (often with a timeworn look), pine furniture, floral chintz fabrics and faded rugs. Accessories often include pieces of delicate floral china as well as a Staffordshire dog or two.

• **French Country.** Pieces in the provincial style are typically crafted of pine or fruitwood, with carving adding eye-catching detail. Armoires, bergères (closed-arm chairs) and fauteuils (open-arm chairs) are some of the signature furnishings. Toile fabrics and café-style curtains further enhance the look.

• **Scandinavian Country.** With its painted wood furniture, bare wood floors and hallmark blue-and-white color scheme (on furniture and fabrics alike), this style is both crisp and calming.

• **American Southwest.** Influenced by Spanish and Native American cultures, Southwest interiors are instantly recognizable by rough-hewn furniture, Navajo rugs and accessories such as pottery that reflect the rich heritage.

above left · This rugged four-poster, made cozier with plaid curtains, is the centerpiece for a room that conveys sophisticated mountain-country style. Masculine elements, like the bed and generously sized chair, team up with more feminine items, such as painted storage pieces, to create a space that's comfortable for both genders.

above right · Ladder-back chairs in this dining area have the same country appeal as the ticking stripes on the armchairs beyond. This black-and-white version of the material teams up with another translation; the fabric used for the bow window treatment is reminiscent of the ticking once used for bed pillows.

left · Windsor chairs, such as these bow-back versions, represent quintessential country style. A wooden table in a lighter tone allows the chairs' profiles to be fully appreciated, while a wrought-iron chandelier spotlights the setting.

ELEMENTS OF STYLE

Country

- Lawson-style sofas with rounded arms
- Windsor chairs
- Medium to light woods, such as oak and pine
- Trestle and rustic, farm-style tables
- Four-poster beds
- Homespun fabrics
- Ruffled skirts on upholstered seating pieces
- Casual curtains
- Braided and hooked rugs

Country Cookin'

Some of the best country interiors have evolved over time—or, at least, they have that look. Furnishings and accessories appear to have been picked up here and there, judging by the mismatched chairs, chests with peeling paint, and pieces of lace worn around the edges. It's a comfortable, put-your-feet-up look that's welcoming.

This kitchen adheres to one of the steadfast rules of country design: It's the heart of the home, so it is large enough to accommodate lots of family and friends. An oversize island takes center stage here, with room for one cook or a whole kitchenful. And nearby there's an extra-deep window seat, the ideal spot to curl up with a cup of coffee or chat with a friend over a glass of wine. There's even a small chandelier hanging from the beamed ceiling, providing a soft source of light in this corner.

But it's the casual eating area that gives this room its undeniable sense of country style. A down-to-earth table with a sturdy iron base is surrounded by a variety of chairs. Some are finely finished, while others show their wear; each, though, has its own distinct personality and, together, add one-of-a-kind character to the space. It's a setting that invites you to linger long after a meal is done.

right • Set atop a base cabinet, a cupboard with tall glass doors has the look of an antique piece. The first clue that it isn't lies inside; the interior of the cupboard is painted the same soft green as the island cabinetry.

left · This casual eating area is an example of country design at its most unpretentious best, with mismatched pieces paired together. The tone of the pieces feels similar, helping to bring cohesiveness to the space.

below · The sense of spaciousness in the kitchen comes not only from the size of the floor plan but also from the high ceilings. The strong vertical reach is emphasized by the entry doors and grandfather clock, but exposed beams help to keep the space from feeling too lofty.

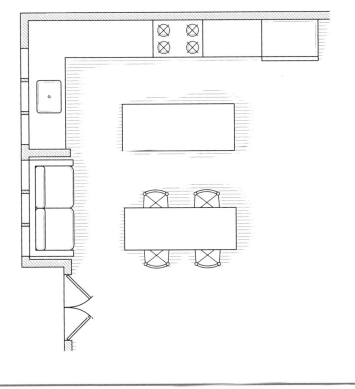

CONTEMPORARY CHIC

While there is technically a distinction between modern and contemporary interiors, the two are often combined into a single category. There are many versions of modern style, including chrome-and-glass furnishings from the 1920s and amoeba-like pieces of the 1940s and 1950s. And, in many cases, the designers' names are just as well known as the iconic pieces themselves. Mies van der Rohe, Le Corbusier and Marcel Breuer were among the European masters of the early 20th century, and their work is still highly respected today. Their American counterparts, whose work first appeared just a few years later, include Charles Eames, Harry Bertoia and Eero Saarinen.

Today's contemporary interiors have continued to evolve over the years. In the 1970s, for instance, the style was so minimalistic that it often incorporated industrial materials. Although the look is still under-stated, it now has a distinctly softer edge. Best of all, today's "softer" contemporary pieces are easier to live with, more comfortable, and more comforting. And there's another plus: They blend better than ever with other furniture styles, allowing you to live with just the amount of contemporary styling you want.

top and bottom • With frilly bed curtains this bed would have taken on a traditional look but with flat panels of fabric forming the canopy it's clearly contemporary. The nearby white chest is just as clean-lined, keeping things simple yet sophisticated.

facing page top • Design continuity is always important but nowhere more so than in combination spaces. This kitchen/dining/living area features charcoal-gray seating in each designated section; the color jumps from a sofa to dining chair and on to counter stools.

facing page bottom • This contemporary conversation area is defined by an alcove-within-an-alcove effect; the middle section is painted a cream color, framed by a warm gray and then creamy walls again. The neutrals provide a striking contrast for the richly colored seating pieces.

Contemporary

- Clean-lined seating, covered in solid fabrics so the styling stands out
- Modular sofas
- Metal tables, often with glass tops
- Platform beds
- Understated window treatments, such as simple fabric shades
- Hardwood floors topped with shag rugs or modular carpet squares

Contemporary Style in an Open Floor Plan

City lofts have become increasingly popular, their oversize windows and soaring ceilings lending the spaces to contemporary style. But more often than not, it's up to the furnishings to assign specific room labels. This conventional loft proves the point. A long and narrow space accommodates living and dining areas as well as a small-scale kitchen; only a narrow wall at one end of the cooking spot provides any division of the floor plan at all. Adjacent to the kitchen, a long, narrow table gives the sense of a separate dining room. So as not to crowd the space, however, chairs are arranged on only one side. (More can quickly be pulled out of storage whenever the need arises.) Further defining the space is a trio of stainless-steel pendant lights, lined up to reflect the shape of the table itself.

The opposite end of the space, dedicated to conversation and home entertainment, is set apart not only by a specific furniture arrangement but also by a red accent wall. The change of color tells you immediately that you've entered a new area. Additionally, the hue warms things up; rooms with all-white walls—especially those with high ceilings that give them more size—can leave you cold. And color is an important element on the opposite side of the room, too. Stair-stepped storage, which conceals entertainment equipment, leaves an opening for a vibrant work of art to become an integral part of the arrangement.

above • While a rug helps define the main conversation area, the absence of one in the adjacent dining space does the same for that space.

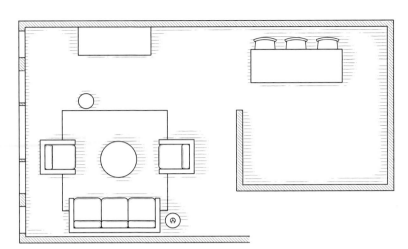

above · Subdued neutrals stand out against this rich red wall, bringing more attention to the contemporary pieces, including a pair of armchairs with strong horizontal lines thanks to their aluminum frames.

right · These storage pieces, with their light finish, were chosen so they wouldn't jut out into the room's traffic pattern or—in this relatively narrow space—visually appear too large. A well-placed work of art, however, keeps the grouping from becoming too inconspicuous.

ECLECTIC SENSIBILITIES

Truth be told, most of us probably fit into the eclectic category, encompassing a mix of furniture styles. After all, whose tastes don't evolve and change? And it's certainly less than practical to throw out everything and start from scratch every time you want to breathe new life into your décor.

Happily, eclectic interiors provide the perfect solution. You can have a variety of styles in a given room and create a cohesive scheme at the same time. In fact, it's one of the best ways to establish a true sense of personal style. But that doesn't mean you can put just anything together, either. There's a secret to successful eclectic interiors, one that today's top designers know well: There must be a common thread that weaves throughout, such as color, form, or scale. Color may seem the most obvious. In a dining room, for instance, you might surround a contemporary table with wooden chairs in a variety of styles— all painted blue. If you go this route, then repeat the blue hue in at least two more places throughout the room. Or mix furniture styles in your living area, but tie them together with an overall creamy color scheme. Take it a step further and accessorize the room with a treasured collection of any sort; the light, neutral backdrop will showcase it beautifully.

Make sure, too, that your major pieces of furniture all have clean, classic lines—no extraneous embellishments that might prove to be a distraction once all of the diverse styles come into play. You will likely be surprised how "at home" dissimilar pieces can be together.

top • The vanity in this master bath is best described as "updated" or "new" traditional style. But the nearby freestanding cabinet is pure country, right down to the peeling paint. It adds personality to the room but also has a practical purpose: The storage piece keeps towels close at hand.

bottom • In its simplest form, an eclectic scheme can comprise just two furniture types. That's exemplified here: An upholstered bed with contemporary styling stands next to a nightstand and lamp with more traditional overtones.

Although the arms of the host and hostess chairs give away their traditional roots, their skirted styling—and that of their armless counterparts—gives them a go-with-anything quality. They comfortably pull up to a traditional table but are equally at home with the nearby Oriental-style armoire.

Eclectic Influence

More and more, today's home is a welcoming haven—a place where families are entertaining family, friends, even colleagues. To that end, the formal dining room, which had all but disappeared just a few years ago, has come back stronger than ever.

This sophisticated scheme is made up of subtle neutrals, punctuated only by colorful accessories here and there. At first glance, there seems to be a contemporary vision, provided by the elegant table and chairs. Upon closer inspection, however, you discover traditional trappings—in the sideboard, a console table, a stunning chandelier. But the two distinct styles work side by side because each piece is classic and can stand on its own design merit. You can clearly appreciate individual elements, too, because this arrangement has sufficient "breathing room"; nothing is so close together that you can't recognize each well-designed form. Even the artwork in this room reflects a diversity of styles. A brilliant contemporary piece takes its place at one end of the room, while a traditional oil painting hovers over the slim console table. It's further proof that, when it comes to design, you really can have it all.

That's not to say that some practical decisions didn't go into this plan as well. The upholstered armchairs, for instance, are a particularly good choice; they're more comfortable for extended periods of time than an armless version.

above · In this eclectic dining room, a traditional chandelier sheds light on a more contemporary table and chairs. The area is underscored by a sisal rug that's neither traditional nor contemporary but a comfortable compromise.

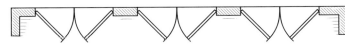

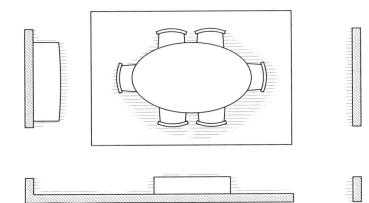

above · Because this dining room also serves as an everyday pass-through, it's important that it has the same relaxed atmosphere as the rest of the house. From a practical point of view, the sisal rug doesn't extend into the traffic pattern, so one side of the floor covering doesn't wear out before the other.

COLOR,

Eye-catching colors, sumptuous fabrics, and irresistible-

to-touch textures — any one or a combination

FABRIC, AND

of all three can transform the most ordinary furnishings

into something extraordinary.

TEXTURE

Color

Starting with the sun's yellow rays that awaken us each morning, color is an ever-present influence. The reds, yellows, and greens of traffic lights guide us to work each day, while the pinks and purples of dusk signal that it's time to go home again. But it's in the home, perhaps, where color is most influential.

Certain colors are associated with specific spaces. Nurseries are predominantly done in pastel hues—if not pale pink or blue then often soft green or yellow. And the cleanliness associated with the bathroom makes pristine white a likely option. But as homeowners become more comfortable with the use of color, personal preferences come into play. Today, you're just as apt to see a baby's room decked out in the colors of the rainbow or a master bath in dark, sophisticated tones. Color choice all depends on your sense of style, the purpose of the room, and the mood you want to create.

The bottom line is that the colors you use should speak to the mood you want to create. You can't help but feel warm and cozy in a red-painted room with a roaring fire, or refreshed in a space done in cool Caribbean blues. More than any other decorative element, color has the power to affect your psyche. And the most important message it should send is "welcome home."

right · **This blue-and-white scheme puts a new twist on traditional style. In lieu of often-used cobalt hues, this room relies on pale pastels; equal parts of the two hues create a relaxing atmosphere.**

top left • Rich red-painted walls energize this living room. Because the high-gloss finish has a distinct sheen—made even more evident by the light coming through the bay window—the backdrop has an extra air of formality.

top right • A girl's room decked out in soft shades of lavender is a refreshing change from the more predictable pink. What's more, this is a color that can grow up gracefully— it's just as appropriate for tot or teen.

above • Shades of yellow, like those in this master bedroom, make any space cheery and bright. Yellow is a particularly good choice in cool, north-facing rooms, where the color creates instant sunshine: Ample doses of white—in patterns and the all-white coverlet—keep the scheme from seeming uncomfortably warm.

PICKING A PALETTE

When looking at a rainbow, it's hard to believe that its colors can be translated in so many ways. Just pick up a paint deck and you'll see how. There are literally thousands of tints and shades available, not to mention the custom colors that you might come up with, too. Even something as simple as white can be found in a wide variety of warm and cool versions.

At first, choosing a color palette for a room might seem intimidating. But it doesn't have to be if you know where to look for clues. Simply think about the specific space and how it will be used:

• Use a hue in the living room that family and guests alike will be comfortable with. Pale peach is a go-with-anything, complementary color.

• Wrap a master bedroom with cool, calming blues or greens; shades should be soft to keep them most soothing.

• Create a play space for the kids using bright, primary colors that have just as much energy as the children themselves.

Most of all, don't overlook hints that may already be in the room. A simple vase may inspire an accent color, while a focal-point rug might be the impetus for an entire scheme. Once you start to think about color from a methodical point of view, you'll find it's more fun than frightening.

top • Seemingly inspired by Mother Nature, this living room is decked out in sunny yellows and spring greens—warm and cool colors that balance each other, bringing the room to a comfortable visual temperature.

bottom • Deep blue, the color of the night sky, makes perfect sense in a room intended for sleep. The dark hue is layered, appearing in varied shades, and accented with touches of warm red that keep the space from becoming too subdued.

Vibrant shades of red—in the patterned banquette, in the solid-color chair cushions, and in the tablecloth—call attention to this casual dining area. The bright hues add a lively touch against the neutral backdrop, creating a convivial mood.

Clear acrylic chairs in this dining room all but disappear, allowing the turquoise blue walls—and the darker shades beyond—to shine through. The contrasting paint colors play up this room's strong geometrical forms, carried through by the contemporary dining table.

above • A soothing shade of green wraps this nursery, with sky blue, appropriately, applied to the ceiling. The solid colors establish a quiet mood, but subtle patterns on the chair and ottoman—as well as the window seat and valance—keep the scheme from falling asleep.

above • Wood tones have inherent warmth, but that characteristic is amplified when they're coupled with a color from the warm side of the spectrum. Without the dark wood peppered throughout the space, the yellow walls and similar-tone floor would have visually faded away

SETTING THE MOOD

Color is emotional, a point proven by the English language itself. Have you ever felt "green with envy"? Heard the phrase "feeling blue"? Every color has its own mood, a feeling that can be translated to a room. Just make sure that the mood you create is appropriate to the space.

• **Red** is dramatic, especially when used in large doses—maybe to paint the dining room walls. In fact, this hue is a good choice for eating areas because it stimulates the appetite.

• **Orange,** in its purest form, can be hard to live with unless toned down with a neutral such as chocolate brown. Still, it adds a sense of warmth, especially when used in its various shades such as terra-cotta, salmon, and coral. Peach is appropriate for living spaces, where you're apt to entertain guests, because it generally flatters skin tones.

• **Yellow** has an inherent sunny disposition, which can quickly warm up a cold, north-facing room. It's energizing and cheery, too, making it a good option for the kitchen.

• **Green,** from the cool end of the color spectrum, is restful and relaxing, particularly in muted forms such as sage. Rich hunter and forest greens are also calming but, at the same time, masculine and traditional, too.

• **Blue** provides serenity, making it a good choice for kitchens and baths. To keep this cool color from turning cold, team it with healthy doses of warm hues like yellow or use it in softer forms such as robin's egg blue.

• **Purple** is associated with royalty and, as such, has a regal feeling. In its strongest form, this hue should be used sparingly so it doesn't overwhelm. Lighter versions, though, such as lavender, can add a softly feminine touch to a bedroom.

right · The red walls in this living room appear even richer thanks to architectural accents in dark neutrals, including the fireplace surround and the ceiling molding. The room's primary colors are picked up in the chairs' upholstery, the stripes providing a tailored look.

below · Wall coverings with bright colors and oversize patterns are best reserved for pass-through spots like this entry, where you can appreciate them but not be overwhelmed. Here, an adjacent library picks up the periwinkle of the hallway and more solidly balances it with lime green.

Creating the Right Feeling

A dining room should be lively, stimulating guests and their appetites. The right color—red—can help set the mood. In fact, color can be used to your advantage to establish any disposition. This yellow room has a sunny temperament, one that gets you up on the right side of the bed every day. The scheme starts with walls painted in the warm color, which gets more intense as daylight streams into the space. From there, the hue repeats in various shades and styles—on a chaise, a side chair, even a floral coverlet. Even the room's all-white elements, like the crisp bed linens, take on a tinge of yellow; thanks to light bouncing off the sunny walls and onto the light neutral furnishings, the room appears more monochromatic than two-tone. The overall effect is soft and soothing, befitting a master bedroom.

above • The linens evident at the foot of the bed—a yellow-and-white coverlet sandwiched between a bright white comforter and a cream-colored upholstered bed—are indicative of the subtle layering of color throughout the room.

below • The pale backdrop of this bedroom makes dark wood pieces—the dressing table, mirror, even the shapely legs of the chair—stand out more distinctly, almost in silhouette style.

USING COLOR IN DIFFERENT WAYS

Whether you tend to be conservative with color or like to spread it around in a big way, there's no end to the variety of ways that color can make a statement. If you're more comfortable with just a few touches here and there, consider a sophisticated scheme made up of subtle neutrals, punctuated by colorful accessories. For instance, accent a camel-colored sofa with decorative pillows in a rich candy-apple red; if you tire of the red accents, it's quick, easy, and affordable to change them out for another color.

To take color to the next level, surround a room with a favorite hue. Drench the walls, and even the ceiling, with a coat of paint. Not only will this approach give you the most bang for your decorating buck, but it's also easy to cover up if you're not satisfied the first time. When considering a paint color for the walls, do yourself a favor and "test" a few shades first. Instead of relying on small paint chips, purchase small amounts of two or three hues (many companies offer sample-size jars), then paint each one on a separate piece of drywall that's at least 2 ft. by 2 ft. Some companies even offer poster-size samples of their paint colors, which you can attach directly to the wall with painter's tape. View the colors in different parts of the room at different times of the day before making your final decision.

right • There was a time when color in the kitchen was relegated to windows and walls. The cabinetry in this kitchen, painted a soft green, enhances the room's cheery attitude. For that matter, painting cabinets any color is a quick and easy way to change the overall tone of a room.

above • A platform bed upholstered in a deep blue is even more eye catching when coupled with crisp white sheets; the contrast better defines the contemporary piece. Behind the bed, an accent wall painted turquoise is in the same color family, keeping the room monochromatic but still providing an unexpected twist.

A profusion of blue-and-white patterns show up on various surfaces in this traditional dining room—on the walls, on the upholstered chairs, even on lamps, pillows, and pottery. While multiple shades of the color are used throughout, it's more important that they blend rather than match exactly.

Take the same approach if you're planning to apply a decorative paint finish. In addition to giving you a good idea of the final effect; it will give you some practice with the technique, too. This small investment in time and money will pay off since there's much less chance that you'll need to repaint an entire room.

If you're truly courageous with color, bring it into a room with a wide variety of fabrics and wall coverings. Wrap the area with a large-patterned wallpaper, then add a mix of complementary patterns in the form of furniture and accessories. Or start with another large expanse such as an area rug or window treatments. A word of caution, however: There can be too much of a good thing. Keep the number of patterns you use somewhere between three and five (it usually takes a pro to work with more than that). And if you use a vast amount of color and pattern, it's equally important to make sure there's a place for the eye to rest so include something like a white pillow or lacy curtains. Plus, the introduction of white will further strengthen the room's other colors.

You can make a strong color statement without a lot of pattern, too. A contemporary space, for instance, can be the perfect canvas for solid shades. Start with bright orange upholstered seating, then underscore the conversation area with a lime green shag rug. Paint the walls a royal blue, then repeat the color in a few accent pieces. The result will be undoubtedly bold, but—if you're comfortable living with it—indicative of a self-assured personality, too.

right · **An easy chair and its accompanying pillow were the inspiration for this colorful bookcase. By simply painting the interior of each separate cube in these two bright hues, and adding a couple of others to the mix, what could have been purely practical becomes eye-popping.**

Coordinating Rooms with Color

A bedroom and bath don't have to be a true suite to come off looking like one—the two rooms will seem as if they were always intended as one as long as there's a common thread of color. In these adjacent spaces, it's merely a matter of playing opposites. In the nursery, green walls provide a quiet backdrop for the light, decoratively painted chest; in the bath, the cabinetry is painted the green color, with the walls taking on the soft neutral hue.

bottom left · Solid colors on this room's upholstered seating pieces allow the shapely forms of each to shine through. When taking this approach, it's important keep the background quiet, in a neutral hue, much the same way one would in an art gallery.

bottom right · Country-fresh decorating is at its best in this dining room, where furniture and accessories all have blue-checked motifs in common. The key to using so much pattern is to balance it with a healthy dose of solid hues, found here in the pickled finish of the table and hutch as well as the blue-painted chairs.

Splashes of Caribbean blue punctuate this living room, drawing the eye from a star-shaped side table to cushy pillows and even a pair of lampshades. The cool color is anchored securely, too; it's repeated at the bottom edge of the window treatments.

Adding Color Punch

If you're unsure of yourself when it comes to mixing colors, simply stick with similar shades, those next to each other on the color wheel. This room is anchored with a bright orange, most apparent on the bed and a nearby chest. A blanket picks up the brilliant hue, but, from there, furnishings step down to less-vibrant tones. For example, a room-size rug brings in a peach color, while the walls introduce a vibrant shade of yellow. Finally, pulling it all together are carefully picked prints, found on decorative pillows, a pair of twin chairs, and an upholstered bench at the foot of the bed. Each fabric is intentionally small in scale, though, so as not to detract from the impact of the room's solid hues.

above • Set against a vivid yellow wall, the cutout areas of this bright orange headboard are just as striking as the painted piece itself.

Any room that's saturated with color needs a strong measure of white to offset the rich hues. Here, crisp white sheets and curtains do the trick, providing a visual resting place for the eye.

Fabric

When it comes to adding character to a room, fabric is just as important as color. The possibilities it provides in terms of pattern and texture bring another dimension to a room. A patterned fabric might provide the springboard for an entire color scheme; likewise, a nubby chenille can add tactile interest, all but irresistible to touch. Whether you love a fine linen in a neutral color or a large-scale cotton floral in brilliant hues, take some time to think about how you're going to use the material before you get too attached to it.

Upholstery fabrics have to wear well. Just how well depends on your own circumstances. Do you have small children? Pets? If so, you'll no doubt need durable and stain-resistant fabrics. When shopping for upholstery fabrics, keep in mind that the higher the thread count (the number of threads per square inch), the more tightly woven the fabric will be and the longer it will last. Conversely, if you're single or if your kids are grown and out of the house, sofas and chairs are likely to get more moderate use, requiring less hardy fabrics. As a general rule, heavy fabrics such as canvas, wool, and leather are more enduring than lighter-weight linen or cotton.

Different factors come into play when selecting fabrics for window treatments. Billowy balloon shades, for instance, call for lightweight fabrics that gather easily. Flat curtain panels, on the other hand, can handle heavier materials. Consider, too, the privacy aspect. Gauzy sheers may be romantic in the bedroom but aren't opaque enough to provide the privacy you need. Either opt for something less transparent or couple them with shades that are less see-through in style.

right • Fabrics with small-scale patterns and prints often "read" as solids, making them easier to mix. This child-size chair and ottoman prove the point, incorporating multiple fabrics that not only work together well but also inspired the room's overall design.

left · The red color found in the artwork over the fireplace translates to a plaid armchair, drawing your eye down from the ceiling and into the conversation group. To further ground the room, the same hue shows up in smaller doses on the sofa and accessories.

bottom left · Repetition of fabrics in a room creates a comfortable rhythm. Here, for instance, a daintily trimmed fabric is used on the valance, then echoed on the skirt of the daybed. Likewise, the coverlet's pattern reappears on the small footstool.

above · To infuse a space with a generous amount of color and pattern, look to large expanses like window treatments. These curtain panels, framing an oversized window, establish a light-hearted mood as well as the room's color scheme.

PATTERN INTERPLAY

Mixing patterns in a room can be as easy as 1-2-3; a good mix can include as few as three basic prints. Choose a large-scale pattern for big pieces such as the sofa, a medium-scale pattern that will work on easy chairs and ottomans, and a mini-print appropriate for pillows and other small items. Likewise, in the bedroom, put the largest pattern on full-length curtain panels, use a medium print for a coverlet, and use a small one to customize a lampshade. All three patterns should have common denominator colors, but they don't have to match exactly. Plus, fabrics should have a similar degree of formality. A fine silk isn't the perfect partner for a homespun gingham but a casual ticking is. If you're unsure of your ability to put together good-looking combinations, take advantage of today's wealth of premixed fabrics; manufacturers have taken the guesswork out of it with precoordinated collections. You'll find them at fabric stores, through online sources, even in wallpaper books, which takes the concept to another level; you can mix and match fabrics with wall coverings, too.

Once you've settled on your three patterns, consider where they will be used in the room. To keep things well balanced, it's best to use each pattern three times— once on a major piece, again on something smaller, then a third time as an accent. For example, the largest-scale pattern might go on the sofa, then be repeated on a table skirt and a decorative pillow. Using patterns in this way will also help create visual rhythm in the room, leading the eye from one design element to the next. Go through the same thought process for all three patterns and, before long, you'll be a master of the mix.

right • A black-and-white toile applied to the walls and repeated on a nearby table skirt creates a romantic ambience in this room. The busy pattern requires balance, though, which is found here in the subtly striped chair.

above • Pale yellow and green fabrics wrap the upholstered pieces in this living room, a small floral print even inspiring the refreshing color of the walls. While the patterned carpet echoes the green hue, it's several shades darker, solidly grounding the scheme.

Bringing the blue of the ocean right through the French doors, this dining room has the same soothing quality as its inspiration point. The chairs' slipcovers make the area comfortable for all occasions; the backs feature a casual plaid fabric, while the fronts are decidedly more formal.

above · The epitome of a well-balanced mix, this bedroom features a small print on the throw pillow and coverlet, a medium-size floral on the chair and ottoman, and an oversize checkerboard floor. The size of each one is well suited to its form, which is key to the success.

Design That's in the Details

Sometimes all it takes is a piece of trim, an embellishment, to inspire an entire room scheme. That's the case in this living room, where an exotic border on the sofa was the impetus for the design direction. The border is applied to the sofa skirt and arms, strategically placed where it can be appreciated most. (It wouldn't have been seen as clearly, for instance, on the sofa's back cushions, where throw pillows or seated occupants would have covered it up.) To further play up the pattern, the rest of the sofa is left pure white, except for snippets of red piping that echo the border's intricate stitching. And the rest of the room? The majority of the pieces are all red or all white, adding to the dramatic impact.

right • Delivering impact with a decorative border or trim can be cost-effective on an upholstered sofa or chair. You'll often spend less for solid-color fabrics used for the bulk of the seating piece.

This color scheme is the result of a simple formula: It's comprised of white upholstery, black-painted wood pieces, and one striking accent—red.

Material World

Before choosing a fabric for your home décor, it's important to know if it suits the situation. Here are some of today's most popular options:

- **Brocade**—This fabric is characterized by a raised floral pattern woven right into it. Best for curtains, table skirts, and canopies, it won't stand up to hard wear and tear.

- **Chenille**—Its name, in French, translates to "caterpillar," of which this fabric's deep pile is reminiscent. It's durable enough to be used on sofas, chairs, throws, and pillows.

- **Chintz**—Most commonly found in floral forms, chintz is simply a cotton fabric with a glazed finish. It can be used for almost any type of home décor, from upholstered walls and seating pieces to bed linens and skirts.

- **Damask**—Formal in style, this fabric is identified by its matte pattern woven into a shiny background. It's a good choice for window treatments as well as upholstery that doesn't see daily wear and tear.

- **Mohair**—Although it's luxurious, this plush material is durable, too. Sofas and chairs upholstered in this fabric are sure to wear well.

top · A single pattern can be a great coordinator. In this nursery, two windows in distinctly different styles called for diverse treatments. Because both are made from the same fabric, though, there's a clear sense of continuity.

bottom · When using just two principal patterns, look for a pair of the same approximate scale. Try to use similar amounts of each as well so your eye sees the total effect at once and isn't drawn to one or the other.

In this bedroom, the wall covering and comforter may not be in matching colors, but their similar paisley motifs give them common ground just the same. They have the same intensity, too, which helps them work well together.

Texture

It may not seem quite as glamorous as color or pattern, but texture is essential to any room. Textures add an element of pattern in their own right: Think of nubby chenilles and coarse linens, smooth tile, and rough-hewn wood. Whether you realize it or not, texture greatly affects the interplay of light and, in turn, how you view your colors and surfaces. Furnishings with shiny surfaces bounce light right back into the room and seem brighter in the process, whereas those with a matte finish absorb light and appear more subdued.

Nowhere, though, is a combination of textures more important than in a room decked out in neutral hues. Consider a room with seating pieces covered in white cotton fabrics and curtains made of the same material; it might even have a wooden coffee table and hardwood floor with similarly smooth surfaces. While each element in its own right has style, together they can create a space that's boring. But with just a few changes, you can change the same room's status to exciting by replacing the white cotton on the seating pieces with a more coarsely textured linen, changing out the plain curtains for a white-velvet stripe and adding a nubby area rug, such as a felted wool shag, beneath the coffee table. Couple hard objects with soft, rough with smooth, and rustic with refined and your reward will be a room rich in design—and diversity.

right • Textures are most apparent—and most needed— in neutral color schemes. Here, a velvety sofa stands out against the coffee table, with its high sheen. Even the contemporary lamp is a study in contrasts, its linenlike shade set atop a wooden base.

left and below • In this living room, vivid colors and patterns catch your attention first, but textures add another layer of visual interest. Shiny mirrors, high-gloss paint, wooden tables, and chenille fabrics are all part of the master textural plan.

above · The rectangular tiles of this bathroom wall offer smooth and rough textures at the same time. The tiles are smooth as glass, but set in grout they collectively have a rippled effect.

above · Textures are varied throughout this living room, but the greatest punch comes from the patterned ceiling. Its strong visual impact draws the eye upward, making the room appear taller in the process.

Adding Visual Interest

Whether you have a neutral scheme in dire need of texture or simply want to add more visual interest to a room, there are a number of ways you can incorporate this element of design:

- If ceiling space allows, add rough-hewn beams overhead.

- Soften a hardwood floor with a shag rug.

- Add a lightweight wicker or rattan chair to your living room, ready to pull up to any conversation grouping.

- Replace an overhead light fixture with a decorative chandelier.

- Add chenille or corduroy pillows to a smooth leather sofa.

- Trim a table skirt with braid or brush fringe.

- Add decorative tassels to curtain tiebacks.

- Drape a fleecy throw over a chair or chaise in the bedroom.

above · Varied textures are never more evident than when two items of the same color but different finishes stand side by side, like this sofa covered in a soft fabric and a wooden chest in a similar hue.

Wicker furniture has a distinct texture all its own, but it's even more prominent in this situation since the pieces have been painted a soft teal blue.

Incorporating Texture

A variety of textures and finishes is a treat for the eye in this country kitchen. More than that, though, they help define the different work zones; the sheer size of this space might have seemed cavernous had it not been visually divided. Around the perimeter of the room, base cabinets are painted a glossy white, blending quietly into the backdrop of sunny yellow walls. To the right of the sink, a hutch is set directly on top of the counter. Used in lieu of conventional wall-hung cabinets, its contrasting wood finish makes it a standout, while glass doors let you quickly find a particular plate or serving piece.

In fact, woods deliver much of the warmth of this room. Species vary throughout the space; some are rough-hewn, while others are polished practically smooth. In the dining area, for instance, a light pine table contrasts with darker ladder-back chairs. And coarsely cut beams have a completely opposite finish than the smooth cabinets that make up the island below. The work area's marble top, stainless-steel appliances, even the white-painted beadboard ceiling all come into play in creating an eye-catching mix in this kitchen.

Like any other well-designed space, however, there's a single ingredient that ties everything together. Here it's the wooden floor, stenciled in a harlequin pattern. With contrasting light and dark hues, it relates to every element in the room.

top · This island includes an overhang at one end, just big enough to accommodate one pull-up chair. It's the perfect place to sit and talk to the cook or spread out with the evening's homework.

bottom · This kitchen is an example of eclecticism at its best. An antique plate rack and a new commercial stove, for instance, are right at home together, side by side.

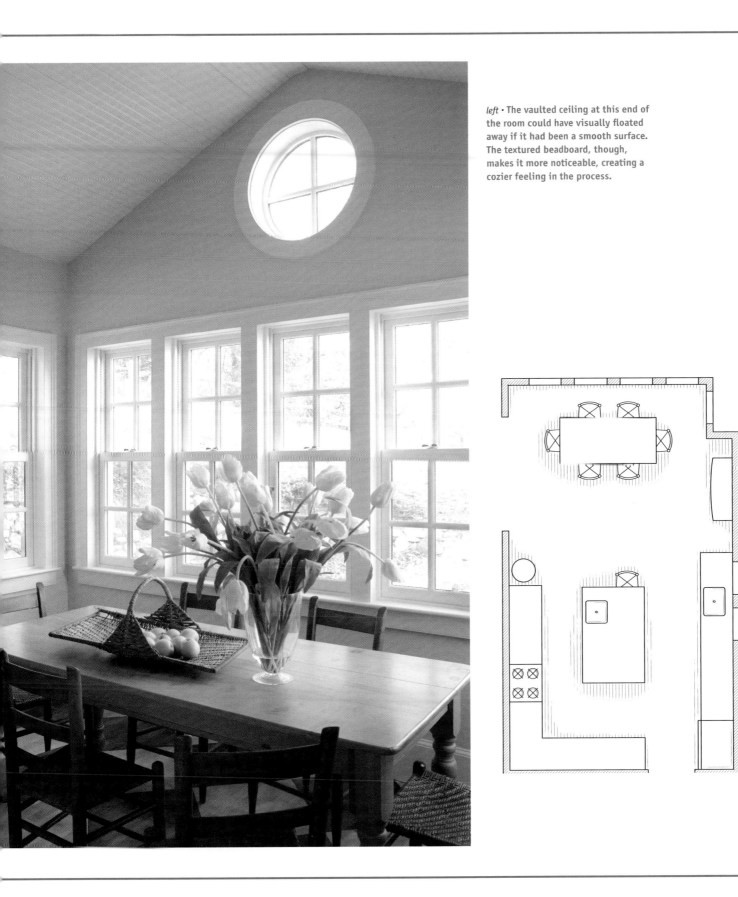

left · The vaulted ceiling at this end of the room could have visually floated away if it had been a smooth surface. The textured beadboard, though, makes it more noticeable, creating a cozier feeling in the process.

WALLS

More than anything else, wall and window

coverings can set the tone for your décor.

AND

They can provide a quiet canvas, allowing the furniture to take

center stage, or be a springboard for the overall color scheme.

WINDOWS

Wall Coverings

There was a time when wall covering choices boiled down to just two—paint and wallpaper. But now options run the gamut of anything that can be applied to a vertical surface. Fabric, wood, and mirrors are used on a regular basis. Even today's wallpapers and paints are showing up in new forms and fashions; the former may be easy-to-apply decals, while the latter might look like leather or suede.

Your wall covering choice should be based on both fashion and function. If the furniture in the room is quietly neutral, you can be more adventurous with color and pattern. Conversely, you'll want something more subdued if the room's major pieces make strong statements of their own. Maintenance will come into play as well, especially if there are children in the family; those inevitable fingerprints, for instance, can be removed more easily from scrubbable paints than they can from fine fabrics.

PAINT

Paint is the great chameleon of wall coverings. You can make a bold statement with a solid hue or create a highly decorative finish, from simple sponging and combing to more elaborate graphic applications— variegated stripes, undulating waves, even gridlike boxes. When purchasing paint, keep in mind that you'll get what you pay for. A high-quality paint will typically last twice as long as its less-expensive counterpart, especially if it's applied with the right primer, which will make the paint go on smoother and provide better coverage, too. Among other considerations is the level of sheen you'll need. Some types, such as semigloss, are easier to clean than others.

right • There's no reason a bathroom can't be as decoratively appealing as any other room in the house. This one, wrapped with a combination of ceramic tile and wallpaper, features the same kind of appealing art grouping you'd find anywhere else.

facing page top · The variegated stripe of this wall covering gives the room extra dimension. This kind of backdrop also makes it easy to bring in other shades of blue—almost any one you come up with is already a part of the pattern.

below · Although this work of art makes a statement on its own, the drama is doubled by the deep chocolate brown wall behind it. The dark hue visually advances, too, seemingly squaring up this long and narrow room.

Choosing the Right Paint

If you're just starting to shop for paint, finding the right kind can be confusing. Oil-based paint is one possibility, but if you don't have professional experience, it's best to stick with latex (water-based) paint. Latex is not only easier to use but also easier to clean up. Even within the category of latex paint you'll find several options—flat, eggshell, satin, semigloss, and high gloss. The various finishes range from matte to shiny, and the washability gets increasingly easier, too. As a general rule, an eggshell finish is best for walls and semigloss for moldings and trim. They'll both give a moderate amount of sheen yet can still be wiped free of fingerprints.

When selecting paint, be mindful of how certain shades can affect your overall scheme. Light colors can make a room seem more spacious than its actual dimensions, while dark hues visually advance, cozying up a space in the process. Even if you opt for basic white or beige, closely compare the alternatives; almost any paint store will offer at least a dozen options, all with varying degrees of warm or cool undertones.

Once you've pared your paint choices to two or three, take a look at them in the intended space. (If you can't find the exact shade you're looking for, ask your paint dealer to create a custom blend; he can match almost anything.) Most manufacturers now offer large paint chips, some even the size of posters. Plus, in-store and online programs allow you to virtually paint your room with the color of your choice. Still, though, the best test is to buy quarts or sample sizes of a few select shades, paint them on 2 ft. by 2 ft. pieces of foamcore or drywall, and observe them on different walls at different times of the day.

A little homework will keep you from purchasing too much paint—or too little. Measure the perimeter of your room and multiply the total by the wall height, which will give you the square footage of the walls. (Don't deduct for windows, doors, or other openings unless they add up to more than 100 sq. ft.) If you want to paint the ceiling, too, multiply the width times the length to get the number of square feet and divide by the number of square feet that a gallon of paint will cover (this is typically 350 to 400 sq. ft., but check your specific brand for accuracy). Round up to the nearest gallon, and then double it to accommodate two coats of paint—sufficient for almost any room.

above • In lieu of a decorative paint technique that's complicated, opt for one that only looks complex. This hallway features simple square motifs painted next to one another in varying shades, giving them all more importance.

Combining Wall Coverings

Diverse wall coverings can be compatible, as proven in this contemporary dining space. On three walls, taupe wallpaper with a subtle texture provides a quiet backdrop. Although it's beautiful in its own right, it's used to set up the accent wall at the end of the room as the real attention getter. Here, sage green and dusty blue stripes are painted horizontally, the green obviously taking its color cue from the marble fireplace façade. Similarly, curtain panels are decked out in stripes; this time, however, they're smaller and pick up the blue and taupe hues. As much as the common colors help to tie the room together, it's the variety of scale that makes it work. The small motif of the wallpaper, medium-size design in the curtains, and oversize stripes on the accent wall lead your eye around the room easily.

right · The pattern of this wall covering may be subtle but its impact is dramatic. It takes on a textural quality, especially against a shiny mirror and mercury-glass accents on the mantel.

below · To strengthen the impact of the painted wall at the far end of the room, assorted furnishings echo its colors, the glass chandelier repeating the green and the relaxed Roman shades resonating with the blue.

Decorative Paint Treatments

To give a room an extra decorative element, use paint to create special finishes. With the help of how-to information (both in brochures and on the Internet) or classes offered by home centers, you can master a technique in practically no time at all.

1. By painting walls using a sueded technique, as in this living room, you get the same effect as the more expensive material at a fraction of the price. 2. Opposing walls get the benefit of a graphic treatment. It's a trendy look, but, because it's done in paint, it can be covered up later. 3. This example of trompe l'oeil (which in French means "fool the eye") adds dimension—and seemingly size—to this bath. This is one decorative technique that's best left to professionals. 4. Clouds painted on the ceiling of a nursery can provide a soothing touch for babies looking up from their cribs. Because no two clouds are alike, you can't go wrong creating them. 5. A two-tone sponged finish applied to this fireplace surround gives the architectural element even more importance.

WALLPAPER

It's no surprise that wallpaper is perennially popular—there's a style and price range to suit everyone. Recent innovations, too, have multiplied the options. In addition to conventional "papers," you'll find murals featuring oversize images—a single rose that covers the entire wall, for instance. Also available are easy-to-apply wall decals (in motifs that appeal to all ages), textured wall coverings that can be painted the color of your choice, even "interactive" wallpapers that arrive with their decorative motifs merely outlined in black and it's up to you how much—or how little—color you want to add to the pattern.

If your walls are smooth, almost any wallpaper will do the job. Cracking or peeling walls, however, call for a heavier paper or at least a liner used with a lighter one. Wallpapers with texture or pattern can also mask the imperfections of the surface beneath. A few good textural choices include grasscloth, foil, and some vinyls. Or, you might opt for paper that simulates the look of wood, leather, or even mosaic tile.

To find out how much wallpaper you'll need for your room, measure the perimeter of the room and multiply the total by the wall height, which will give you the square footage of the walls. If you're covering the ceiling, too, multiply its width times the length to get the number of square feet. Divide the total by 25, the average square footage that you'll get out of a standard single roll of wallpaper, and subtract a half roll for each window or door. When purchasing wallpaper, keep in mind that the pattern and "run numbers" are printed on each roll; different dye lots vary slightly, so make sure that all of your rolls are from the same run and that you buy a sufficient amount the first time. You can always return an extra roll—or find other creative ways to use it. Also take into account any pattern match; more wallpaper is required if you're working with a large motif.

above • Pastel gingham patterns are playful, which makes them a particularly good choice for this kids' bath. Two different colors define separate spaces, with the common motif making them work as one.

above • Red is a color often used in Oriental-style settings. This grasscloth wall covering adds a layer of texture next to window treatments in the form of shoji-like screens.

A blue-and-white paisley wall covering creates a refreshing and relaxed mood in this room. Because it's on the light side, the covering provides a striking contrast for the dark-wood bed, silhouetting every curve of its design.

Border Lines

Borders can serve any number of purposes. They can be purely decorative, adding a design element to an otherwise plain wall. They can run along—or just below—the ceiling line, providing a stopping point for the eye on an extra-high wall. They can even take the place of a conventional chair rail, allowing you to decorate the upper and lower portions of a wall in different ways.

1. A tile border runs right "through" this bathroom mirror, tying the two together. Directly below, a smaller-scale border underscores the effect. 2. Many of today's wallpaper patterns have coordinating borders like this one, taking the guesswork of mixing and matching out of the equation.
 3. Painted just below the ceiling level, this stenciled border is right in keeping with the room's established Arts and Crafts theme. 4. In this laundry room, a tiled backsplash protects the walls but the whimsical "line" of hanging clothes is what adds decorative impact.

FABRIC

Sometimes overlooked as a wall covering option, fabric can cover up less-than-perfect walls or simply make a dramatic statement. Fabric can complement traditional or contemporary interiors and can be used on a single wall or in an entire room.

Unlike wallpaper, fabric can be applied in a variety of ways, depending on whether you're interested in practicality or pure aesthetic appeal. It can be applied flat—letting you fully appreciate the pattern—gathered, or even pleated. If good looks are your goal, you can apply a favorite fabric with adhesive or staple it right onto the wall once you've added furring strips (which the fabric attaches to). Simply seam the material so it reaches the entire width of the wall, matching pattern repeats as you go. Furring strips should be spaced the same width as each panel so you can conceal staples along each seam. At ceiling and floor levels, as well as at the corners, staples are more likely to show; you might want to hide them with decorative braid or cord. For a softer look, gather the fabric on rods attached to the top and bottom of the wall or, for a more free-flowing, curtain-like look, at the top only. This technique—referred to as shirring—requires more fabric, though, since each panel should be three times the width of the wall to achieve the right amount of gathers. For pleated walls, you'll also need three times the fabric, but it should be stapled onto furring strips, too.

To add an aspect of function to each of these methods, put a layer of batting down first, then cover it with either flat or shirred fabric panels. Not only will this provide heat and sound insulation but also the wall's imperfections will be hidden. Or, take a cue from the Victorian era and curtain off a doorway; when privacy is a priority, you can simply pull the curtains shut. By the same token, you could suspend a floor-length curtain from a rod affixed to the ceiling, using it to partition off a room—an idea that's often used to perfection in spaces such as city lofts.

above • Creamy white fabric shirred along the far wall of this bedroom not only softens the space but also creates a secondary "headboard." It lends another texture, differentiating it from the room's other neutral hues.

above • This red-and-white traditional fabric was applied directly to the wall. For this technique, the walls must be carefully prepared first; unless they're completely smooth, even the smallest imperfection will show.

This niche is a natural place to put a bed; it easily accommodates the sleeping spot, creating the equivalent of a built-in canopy. To give it more attention, the back wall is covered with a plaid fabric, a sharp contrast to the wall covering throughout the rest of the room.

Wall Coverings

With so much surface space to offer, walls are a natural to set the tone of a room. Making the right choice will put you well on your way to creating a space that's infused with personal style.

PAINT
$

- Inexpensive; easy to apply
- Offered in a wide variety of colors; custom mixes also available
- Semigloss and high-gloss finishes are easy to clean
- Some types of paint will off-gas volatile organic compounds (VOCs); low-VOC and no-VOC paints are available but are more expensive
- Manufacturers offer some pre-coordinated color schemes, taking the guesswork out of it
- Decorative tools and techniques are available to create custom wall treatments

WALLPAPER
$$

- Available in a wide variety of colors and patterns
- Manufacturers precoordinate many prints with borders and even fabrics
- Relatively easy to apply
- Depending how permanent the adhesive is, it can be difficult to remove

WOOD
$–$$

- Comes in a variety of forms, from sheet goods to tiles
- Can be painted, stained, or given a clear-coat finish
- Look-alikes are available for some types, such as traditional beadboard
- Real wood should not be used in high-humidity areas

TILE
$$–$$$

- Very durable
- Impervious to water when installed with well-sealed grout; a good choice for kitchens and baths
- Vast assortment of textures, colors, and sizes provides design flexibility
- More expensive than other wall coverings

FABRIC
$$–$$$

- Available in an endless assortment of patterns, textures, and colors
- Can be applied in flat panels, gathered, or pleated
- When batting is applied between wall and fabric, it makes a good sound and temperature insulator
- Because large amounts of yardage are required, it can be expensive

PAINT

CERAMIC TILE

WALLPAPER

WOOD TILE

GLASS TILE

TILE

Although wall tile is most often associated with the kitchen and bath, there are plenty of other possibilities, too. In addition to the more expected backsplashes and tub surrounds, it can be used to create striking wainscoting, frames for bathroom mirrors, even fireplace façades. Wall tiles differ from their floor counterparts in that they're typically thinner; check the manufacturer's guidelines to make sure you're getting the appropriate product. Beyond that, the characteristics are similar. Wall tiles can stand up to high moisture and are easy to wipe down with the rest of the room. And the decorative options know no bounds. Ceramic tiles, in myriad colors, patterns, and textures, are most common. Glass mosaics can add sparkle to a space; some tiles even have metallic finishes. Plus, you'll find marble tiles in a wide range of rich hues.

Whether you're tiling a small area or making a statement on an entire wall, you can use a variety of shapes, patterns, and colors to create a striking field—the main area you're tiling. Consider accent or border tiles as well to provide the finishing touch. Although tile is more expensive than most other types of wall coverings, you can keep the cost down by scattering pricey handmade varieties or a narrow band of mosaic glass throughout a solid-color less-expensive field tile. Don't assume that white grout is your only option, either. It can be tinted to subtly blend into the background or in a contrasting color for an entirely different look.

top · **The pattern and texture presented by this backsplash enliven the neutral-colored kitchen. The tile's fluid motifs also provide a welcome change of pace, visually speaking, from the angular lines throughout the rest of the room.**

bottom · **Glass mosaic tiles, used to create a backsplash and a matching tub surround, add a sparkle to this master bath. Giving this room a sense of rhythm, the square shapes are repeated in the glass block window as well as in the tile floor.**

Mirror Images

For grooming purposes, mirrors are essential to any bath. But they can serve another purpose, too. In small rooms mirrors can seemingly double the space when covering an entire wall. Here, a glass vanity with slender chrome legs barely interrupts the mirrored wall at all, allowing it to fully reflect the opposite wall. Additionally, large expanses of mirrors bounce light back and forth throughout a space, brightening it in the process.

below · Two completely different but compatible tiles define separate zones in this master bath. Cut-stone tiles near the vanity area are highlighted by recessed lighting to better spotlight their texture, while smaller and darker mosaics cozy up the tub area.

Tile

Used to define a border, create a backsplash, or cover an entire wall, tile has a combination of characteristics that is hard to beat. Not only is it versatile and durable, but—of all the wall covering options—it's also the easiest to keep clean. Just as important, it fits any budget, since you can use as much or as little as you like.

1. Small gray and white mosaics on the walls of this room replicate the shape of the floor tiles, not to mention the luxurious Japanese soaking tub. 2. Tumbled marble tiles give definition to the backsplash behind this commercial stove. 3. Lavender wall cabinets with cream-colored base counterparts might have been a stretch without some kind of unifying element, provided here by a colorful backsplash that incorporates both colors and many more. 4. Ceramic tile is a logical choice for a shower surround, a concept taken to the max here. Three slightly different tiles coexist beautifully on the walls, floor, and ceiling. 5. The tile in this bath may be in subdued hues, but that doesn't make it any less striking, particularly because the top row was set to extend further into the room, adding extra dimension. 6. A subdued neutral tile teams up with bright tile sticks on the façade of this fireplace, with the latter helping to tie the fireplace to the adjacent red wall.

WOOD

For those seeking the warmth of wood, there's good news. No longer are wood wall coverings limited to traditional paneling or beadboard that lends itself to a cottage-style look. Wood is just as apropos in contemporary interiors, given the lighter shades and wider sheets that are available today.

Wood can be painted, stained, or left in its natural color as long as it's sealed. But if you're planning to leave it in its natural state, be prepared to spend a little more; the best grades of cherry and mahogany, for instance, are expensive. Most traditional wood paneling features elaborately carved detailing and, if sealed with oil or wax, will develop a rich patina over time. Simple tongue-and-groove paneling, in oak or pine, often shows up in country interiors. Grades that have many knots and surface defects are particularly appealing in rustic rooms. And flat expanses of maple or ash have contemporary appeal.

From a practical point of view, keep in mind that wood expands and contracts when exposed to humidity, so it should always be protected from exposure to water. Even when protected by a sealer or paint, wood isn't a good choice for constantly wet areas such as shower walls and tub surrounds. In some cases, however, you can get the same look. If you're fond of white-painted beadboard, for instance, use a PVC product that's similar in style and will stand up to moisture, too.

top · Tongue-and-groove paneling can be painted to give it a new outlook, as in this bedroom. You can find paintable PVC tongue-and-groove sheet goods at home centers, as well, which cost much less than the real thing.

bottom · This dining room looks as though a parquetry floor has been applied to the walls. Sections of wood with well-defined graining alternate back and forth, resulting in a checkerboard-style pattern that's subtle but distinctive, like the rest of the room's furnishings.

Wood-paneled walls are too often assumed to be dark, most appropriate for libraries and masculine home offices. But these have been painted a pale hue, giving this living room a contemporary ambience.

Decorative Screens

A decorative screen can have a purely practical purpose, dividing a large room into two small spaces or simply concealing a storage space. Likewise, it can be purely decorative. Many of today's styles can soften a corner, supply color and texture, and even add architectural dimension to a room. The possibilities are only limited by your imagination.

1. Nearly reaching to the ceiling, this screen—with a blown-up map motif—gives this mini-office a sense of place, literally and decoratively. **2.** While this decorative screen softens a corner of the dining room, it doesn't completely conceal the walls' painted finish, thanks to vertical rows of cutouts. **3.** Embellished with thin, hooplike shapes that match the light wood frame, this mirrored screen takes on a contemporary attitude. **4.** This screen relies on shape alone to create a division of space. It keeps the area from feeling too closed off, since occupants are still able to see beyond. **5.** Wallpaper adds a decorative aspect to this folding screen, which can be assembled with hollow doors, hinges, and the wallpaper pattern of your choice.

TRIM

The right moldings and trim can add visual interest to even the most ordinary room. Cove and crown moldings are often used where the tops of the walls meet the ceiling to draw the eye upward. They can be purchased in preformed pieces at your local home center in wood or polyurethane, the latter of which has the look of plaster. Likewise, they can be painted to match the rest of the room's woodwork, the same color as the walls or ceiling, or in a contrasting hue.

Another commonly used element is a chair rail, typically placed 3 ft. to 4 ft. up from the floor (or about one-third of the way up the wall). The chair rail's original purpose was purely practical; it kept chair backs from scraping against the wall. They still serve the same purpose today but have aesthetic value, too. The area below the chair rail, known as the dado, can be painted, wallpapered, or even paneled, and is referred to as wainscoting; the portion of the wall above the rail can be treated in a complementary fashion. Likewise, a piece of molding might be placed at dish-rail height, approximately 2 ft. from the ceiling. In this case, the areas above and below the rail can be treated the same or in a complementary way. If the covering you use below the dish rail has strong vertical lines—beadboard, for instance—it will draw the eye from floor to ceiling and make the room seem taller in the process.

right • There's something refreshing about splashing a bath with large quantities of white. That's evident in this room, where the dado—the area beneath the chair rail—consists of white beadboard, which matches the baseboard, window trim, and chair rail itself. As a complementary color, what could be more appropriate than watery blue?

above · The real beauty of trim is that it lets you customize in endless ways, as this trimmed-out corner of a kitchen proves.

left · In contemporary settings such as this, crown molding and other trim is typically white. But here, by playing up the wood's natural dark hue, the effect is markedly more dramatic, especially set against the pale finish of the walls.

Moldings

The right moldings can transform a space, taking even the most basic box and turning it into an architectural beauty. You'll find them in wood, plaster, and synthetic forms, but all will add an element of visual interest.

CROWN MOLDING

Creates an architectural transition between the wall and ceiling

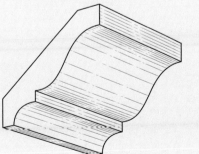

CHAIR RAIL

Horizontal band located approximately one-third of the way up a wall

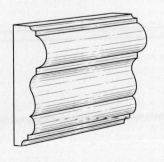

BASEBOARD

Serves as a transition between the wall and floor

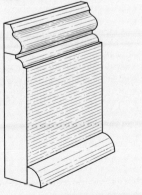

Ceilings

If you count the walls in your room and come up with four, look up and count again. The ceiling, or fifth wall, provides another decorative opportunity. Something as simple as painting the ceiling a shade darker than the walls can create a cozy feeling. A pale hue (but not white) will seemingly raise the surface, making the space seem taller in the process. Or, if you're feeling daring, make it a contrasting color. In a room with a floral wall covering, pull out the least-apparent hue and splash it across the ceiling to lend an element of surprise. To make the look as seamless as possible, take the time to paint air registers and the bands of recessed lights, as well.

The painted approach is a good one for ceilings, but it's by no means the only alternative. Use a wallpaper on the ceiling that complements the one used throughout the rest of the room. (Today's premixed wallpaper collections make it easier than ever to coordinate.) Opt for pressed tin or a wall covering that replicates it. Or cover just a square of space in the center and border it with wood trim to imitate the look of a ceiling medallion. Likewise, designate that central section for decorative tile or cover the entire surface with wood. And fabric is just as viable on the ceiling as it is on the walls. Upholster that fifth wall with a rich jacquard fabric or with something more lightweight to create a tented look.

top · This vaulted ceiling could have made the master bedroom appear cavernous. But well-placed trim—painted bright white to stand out against the yellow backdrop—brings it down to earth, the extra dimension seemingly lowering its level.

bottom · Blue-and-white tile is often found in the kitchen—on the backsplash as well as on the floor. Unusual but effective, a similar look finds its way to the ceiling here, creating the same kind of space-defining element as a room-size rug.

Natural materials play an important role in this room, and the ceiling is no different. Rich teak is a handsome complement to the stone-covered wall; carefully mitered at the corners, it's just as exacting as the stone is free-form.

Window Treatments

Depending on personal style, windows can be as dressed up—or dressed down—as you like. A traditionalist might opt for opulent draperies, complete with tassels and trim, while a minimalist may prefer simple roller shades. Before making any fashion statements, though, it's important to consider the practical point of view. Start by asking yourself the following questions:

• What is the purpose of the room? Is it a kitchen, where you want plenty of natural light, or a bath, where privacy comes into play?

• What direction does the room face? If it's a south-facing space, for instance, consider shutters or blinds that can control the sun's strong afternoon rays.

• Are there any special needs? For example, if a family member works the night shift, give some thought to blackout blinds in the bedroom so he or she can sleep during the day.

• How does safety figure into the solution? In children's rooms and nurseries, there should be no operational cords that might cause a safety hazard.

After paring down the list of potential window treatments, having decided what's practical and what's not, your choice becomes a matter of style. Do you want it to be a focal point in the room or blend quietly into the background? Does the window itself have a stunning view? If so, think in terms of a window dressing that will allow Mother Nature's beauty to shine through. The right treatment can even "change" the dimensions of a window. A standard, double-hung style, for instance, will appear taller with curtains that reach all the way to the floor or up to the ceiling. Likewise, a narrow window will seem wider with a longer rod above and an extra curtain panel on either side.

above • Relaxed Roman shades instill a casual feeling. In this bathroom, they also add a faint touch of color, the fabric just a little brighter than the cream-colored cabinetry.

above • Taking a color cue from the bed linens, this window treatment proves that pretty and practical can go hand in hand. Roman shades with decorative headers add color and pattern while handling privacy duties, too. Framing the shades, coordinating curtains can be closed for more complete darkness.

In this bay window, floor-to-ceiling sheers team up with only slightly more opaque tieback curtains, allowing sunshine to stream into the space while still keeping a sense of formality. In the same light neutrals as the sectional sofa, the elements, together, read as one.

DRAPERIES AND CURTAINS

Most people distinguish draperies from curtains by their level of elegance: Draperies are elaborate and formal, while curtains are their informal counterparts. In truth, the differences are more technical. Draperies typically reach to the floor, suspended from cord-operated hardware such as a traverse rod. The panels are lined as a rule and sometimes even interlined (another lining between the primary lining and the decorative fabric), making them hang better and more energy efficient. Curtains, on the other hand, are characteristically lighter in weight and unlined, but they're operable, too. The difference is that you usually open and close them by hand.

Drapery fabrics run the gamut. Velvet, silk, and damask are perfectly suited for the most formal rooms, while linen and cotton are appropriate for spaces that have a more understated elegance. The hardware will affect the overall look, too, whether it's a completely concealed traverse rod or decorative wrought iron with finials. Before purchasing hardware, figure out what your draperies' stackback will be—the width of the window treatment when it's fully retracted (the wider the window, the wider the stackback will be). You'll need to add that figure to the width of your window to find the appropriate rod length; when the draperies are completely open, they should cover the window frame but not the glass. Finally, don't forget about embellishments: Cord, fringe, and tape are details that can truly make a difference.

right · **A close look at the area rug in this room reveals the inspiration for the color scheme. The coral hue permeates the space, most evident in the valance-topped drapery treatment complete with tassel trim.**

Window Hardware

Even though decorative rods support window treatments of all kinds, they by no means settle for supporting roles. Wood finishes continue to be popular as well as metal, including brass, wrought iron, burnished bronze, brushed nickel, aged pewter, and copper. For contemporary interiors, wire rods are another option, whereby lightweight curtains are simply attached to a length of wire with clips. Finials can also make a decorative difference; some rods have preattached finials, while others give you the option of choosing your own.

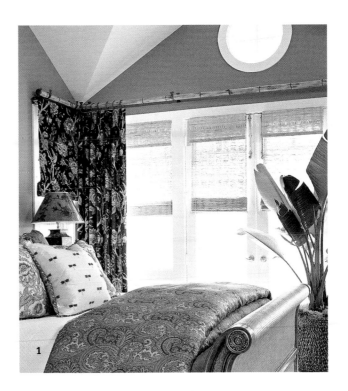

1. Bamboo decorative rod. 2. Wrought-iron holdback. 3. Decorative wooden rod with look-alike metal finish and finial. 4. Metal decorative rod with finial.

Curtains may be more casual than draperies, but they don't give up a thing in terms of style. Light-weight—and, more often than not, unlined—they can be suspended from the accompanying hardware by rings, clips, tie or tab tops, or a rod pocket, reaching just to the windowsill or all the way to the floor. Cottons and linens are good candidates for curtains, and, like draperies, they're often embellished with trim. Or add your own flair by customizing store-bought panels with the trim of your choice.

Sheer curtains, too, are a popular option. They're sometimes used in tandem with more elaborate "overdraperies" but, in today's interiors, are more likely to take the lead role. Dotted-Swiss sheers, for instance, are right at home in a cottage-style setting; coupled with a roller or pleated shade—nearly invisible when completely open—the privacy aspect is covered, too. In addition to white, sheers are now available in a wide variety of pale hues, all in keeping with the light weight of the fabrics, including gauzy cottons, filmy voiles, and even see-through lace. Many have subtle patterns, too, ranging from geometric plaids and stripes to those with soft, realistic motifs. When fabricating curtains, though, keep the styling just as simple as the fabric itself—its delicate nature isn't strong enough to stand up to styles with complex pleats and folds.

right · **Country cottage style is typically colorful, with large amounts of white thrown in. This bedroom fits the description, right down to the simplified curtains. The tiebacks are intentionally high, in keeping with the soaring ceiling.**

above left · Window treatments used to dress French doors require special consideration. To allow the doors to open, they either need to pull completely to the side—as in this dining room—or pull up over the top of the door frame.

above right · Asymmetrically swagged valances completely change the mood of this room. Had their "tails" been even on both sides, the look would have been as formal as the rest of the room's furnishings. This way, the look is more casual.

left · Sometimes window placement dictates that a bed be arranged directly in front of it. By matching this window treatment to the headboard below, the effect is like that of a canopy, especially when the scalloped shade is pulled down completely.

Window Treatments Create Continuity

It goes without saying that window treatments serve a practical purpose, whether it's providing privacy or filtering the sun's light. And, of course, they're decorative. But they sometimes go beyond double-duty and do triple time by pulling together a room that serves multiple needs, putting a common element in each. This country kitchen is a case in point.

Establishing a blue-and-white color scheme, the treatments start with shirred curtains on the bottom halves of the double-hung windows; made (appropriately) from a windowpane plaid fabric, the curtains are secured by tension rods at both top and bottom. The shirred dressings are framed by coordinating panels which, though simple in style, seem more elaborate thanks to contrasting trim along the inside and bottom edges. In the kitchen, the window treatments reach from near the ceiling to the countertop; in the dining area, all the way to the floor. Additionally, at this end of the room, their height provides the framework for a tall cupboard, perfectly suited for a sliver of space between two of the windows.

With the blue-and-white theme well established by these treatments, the two colors reappear throughout the room—on cabinetry and lampshades, on pillows and slipcovers, on decorative plates and even the painted floor. It's crisp enough to be smart looking, yet calming enough to put you at ease.

right · **While the kitchen area is predominantly white, the dining area takes the opposite tact; its black furnishings help create a visual separation between the two adjacent spaces.**

above left · Just steps away from the kitchen, two wicker chairs provide a place to plan family meals or share a cup of tea with a friend.

above right · White-painted open shelves on one side of the stove and an unpretentious pot rack on the other are indicative of the laidback approach to this kitchen, which makes it all the more livable.

left · An armchair slipcovered in the same floral fabric as the curtains makes the seating piece blend quietly into the background, a plus in this moderate-size space.

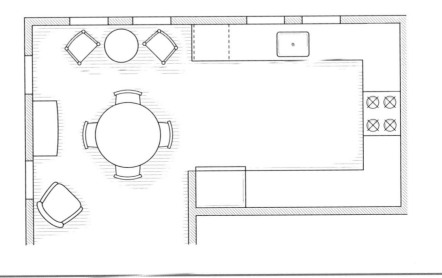

VALANCES AND CORNICES

Valances and cornices were originally intended to serve the same purpose—to conceal the tops of window treatments, hardware and all. Today they still function in the same way, but they're just as apt to be teamed up with blinds and shades (which are completely concealed when open all the way) or used alone as a decorative element.

Valances are softer in style than cornices. They may be shirred or tailored, or even look like balloon or Roman shades when in the up position. Swags and jabots are one of the most traditional—and elegant—options, but a more casual translation of the look can be achieved by simply draping a long, silky scarf over a decorative rod. Mounted on boards (and attached with Velcro®) or on separate hardware of their own, valances are typically 12 in. to 16 in. high. To keep a room's proportions in sync, taller versions should be reserved for spaces with higher ceilings.

Cornices are the wooden counterparts of valances. Fastened directly to the wall with screws, they can take virtually any form. Box shapes are most common, but you'll also find ones with scalloped or saw-tooth edges. To make them more architectural, moldings can be added, too. Cornices can be painted or stained to complement the accompanying window treatment or the overall room décor; for a more decorative look, they can be covered with wallpaper or wrapped in fabric.

right • In a kitchen, a valance is often all that's needed; there are no privacy issues, and it's a bonus to have sunshine pouring into the space. Another advantage: With these short window treatments, there's less danger of splattering food on them.

above • A wooden cornice can blend seamlessly into the molding at the ceiling level. This one crowns a pleated window treatment that, when closed, creates the effect of a headboard.

top · If you like the look of a balloon shade, but know that it will remain in the up position, opt for a stationary balloon valance.

above · A pleated valance can sometimes be seen as too tailored for a child's room. In this case, however, bows at the top of each pleat and contrasting trim along the bottom give it a youthful appearance.

left · This window treatment takes the layered look to the nth degree. A white pleated shade provides privacy, while a valance (which conceals the shade's hardware) carries out the room's color theme. Over it all, mobile-like strands suspended from the valance add a touch of whimsy.

BLINDS AND SHADES

Blinds and shades have one distinct difference: Blinds have moving parts while shades do not. The former includes horizontal and vertical blinds, which can be closed for privacy or opened to allow light into a room. The latter, on the other hand, comprises Roman shades, balloon shades, roller shades, and woven shades made of natural materials such as reeds and exotic grasses.

Shades provide both light and privacy—and more color and pattern possibilities than blinds. Standard *roller shades* are the most basic option, but even they have gone beyond their once all-white norm. They're now available in myriad styles with custom hems, trims, and pulls. *Pleated* or *cellular shades* are also perennially popular. Because they hang so close to the window, they're good insulators. Plus, when completely raised, they all but disappear. For the best of all worlds, window *shadings* offer a cross between a blind and a shade; opaque fabric slats between two layers of sheer fabric can be tilted to control light and privacy. *Woven shades* are made from natural fibers, such as bamboo, that have been woven together with a heavy thread. Any of these options can be used on their own or under a more decorative window treatment.

Balloon or *Roman shades* are more likely to make a design statement on their own. Balloon shades typically feature evenly spaced inverted pleats that billow out at the bottom. Some, however, have shirred headers; these balloon shades have even more romantic appeal, with soft gathers at both bottom and top. On the contrary, Roman shades have a more tailored look. These classic window coverings can be identified by their crisp folds. Some relaxed versions, though, feature an ever-so-slight swag along the bottom edge.

A balloon shade, by its very nature, falls into soft folds along the bottom edge. A variation on the theme is this London shade, which kicks out into fanlike pleats on either side.

left · Woven shades, made of natural materials, can be used alone or be paired with another soft treatment. They're easy to install and one of the least expensive types of shades you will find.

Unifying Windows in a Room

You have a room with two distinctly different windows. So how can you tie them together? The secret is in fabric choice. The more versatility your fabric has—the ability to be gathered or take the shape of sharp folds—the more options you'll have. A casement window behind this twin bed and nearby French doors presented that challenge, but a pair of prints proved up to the task. A classic Roman shade hangs over the doors, then reappears in back of the bed. Here, though, it teams up with a soft canopy that frames the bed as well as the window.

Horizontal blinds, sometimes referred to as Venetians, are most commonly made of wood, vinyl, or aluminum. Wood options continue to be the most popular, with a wide variety of finishes and decorative tape options. You might, for instance, choose a dark-wood blind and a cantaloupe-colored tape to go on it, to pick up one of the hues in your room. To get the same look in rooms that aren't wood friendly—those that are high in humidity—consider composite wood blinds, which won't crack, fade, or warp. Or consider aluminum and vinyl versions, which come in a wide variety of colors. Vertical blinds, meanwhile, are typically made from vinyl or fabric that's been stiffened to hold its louvered shape.

Tremendous advances also have been made in the mechanics of blinds and shades. Today's cordless varieties let you raise and lower these window treatments by simply pushing or pulling the bottom rail. Still others come with a retractable cord, which remains the same length no matter how much the window covering is raised or lowered. The real bonus that comes with these innovations, though, is the safety factor, especially important in the rooms of infants and toddlers.

above • Vertical blinds are especially impressive when they play up the forms of irregular windows. In this dining room, they lead your eye straight to the ceiling, making it seem higher.

above • This window treatment has the best properties of both blinds and shades. Vanes between two panels of sheer fabric give it the look of a soft shade when open but completely block out light when closed.

above • Horizontal blinds made of wood are particularly fitting for traditional and country schemes. The mechanics—the strings that operate the blinds up and down—are barely detectable between each slat but can be concealed completely with decorative tapes.

Soft Shade Styles

Roman and balloon shades work much the same way—they're raised and lowered via strategically placed tapes on the back of the window treatments. So it really comes down to a matter of style: Balloon shades are billowy while Romans tend to be more tailored.

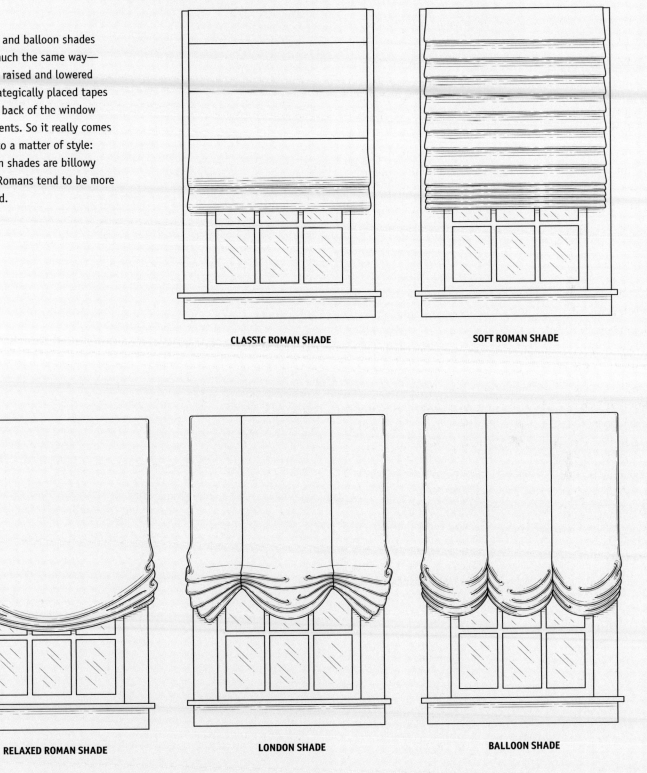

CLASSIC ROMAN SHADE

SOFT ROMAN SHADE

RELAXED ROMAN SHADE

LONDON SHADE

BALLOON SHADE

SHUTTERS

Shutters have enjoyed a renaissance. Today, they're appreciated not only for their practicality but also for their pure aesthetic value. They can be the basis for a striking window treatment, coupled with soft curtains or more elaborate draperies. But shutters can also be a stunning solution in their own right; attached directly to the window frame, they become an integral part of a room's architecture. From a functional point of view, the louvers, when open, allow sunshine to pour into a space. When closed, they're energy efficient and allow complete privacy. Not all shutters are made of wood, either; vinyl alternatives are also available. Plus, they don't only come in white. You'll find shutters in beige, black, and other neutral hues.

Traditional shutters have louvers that measure from 1¼ in. to 1¾ in. that provide optimum privacy. At the same time, they're good insulators for both climate and sound. The narrow louvers, however, will somewhat limit your view. A compromise might be *café shutters*, which cover only the lower half of the window, much like a café curtain. *Plantation shutters* are better suited for large expanses of glass. Most are fitted with louvers that are from 2½ in. to 3½ in. wide. Their large scale provides more drama as well as a better view out when they're opened.

Shutters are not limited to conventional windows. Custom versions can be made to fit any size, including arched and eyebrow windows. For doorways, consider using sliding shutters. They operate on a track, with one door sliding neatly behind the other.

right · Traditional shutters are neatly installed within the window frame itself. As this bedroom proves, today's options go far beyond conventional white; you'll find them in a variety of colors, including this spectacular black.

above · It's no secret that window treatments for sliding or French doors can be nothing short of a challenge. These sliding doors, with inset shuttered louvers, offer a handsome solution.

Plantation shutters have a rich traditional heritage but also a chameleon-like quality, making them at home almost anywhere. Plantations are more expensive than other types of shutters, but they're worth it since they can stand alone on their own design merit.

FLOORS

Floors can add impact to any room in the home. With so many handsome material options, from low budget to high style, flooring that's both appealing and practical is within everyone's reach.

Hard-Surface Flooring

Hard-surface flooring can be divided into two categories—nonresilient and resilient. Under the heading of nonresilient flooring are wood, ceramic tile, stone, brick, and quarry tile. Resilients include vinyl, linoleum, and laminate, as well as cork and rubber. The difference between the two is in how "forgiving" the surface is—resilient is a bit more spongy than nonresilient, so it typically feels better on the feet. Plus if you drop a dish on a resilient floor, it will have a much better chance of surviving the fall in one piece.

WOOD

Wood is the perfect go-with-anything flooring, complementing virtually any décor. It's easy to care for and comes in a wide variety of types. Oak is one of the most common simply because it's readily available, but other popular domestic species include maple, ash, birch, cherry, hickory, pecan, and walnut. If you're looking for something with more rustic appeal, consider recycled or reclaimed lumber; its very age gives it an unbeatable patina. Plus, exotic species are more accessible than ever, such as Brazilian cherry, leopardwood, kempas, purpleheart, and tigerwood.

Hardwoods, such as oak, maple, and cherry, are the most durable species; softwoods, such as pine, will dent more easily. (That can be turned into an advantage, though, if you want a distressed look in a country-style room.) When shopping for wood flooring, be sure to compare not only the species but the also grain. Oak, for instance, has a pronounced pattern that disguises dirt and dents better than woods with more subtle grains. You'll find wood flooring in strips ($1\frac{1}{2}$ in. to $3\frac{1}{4}$ in. wide), planks (3 in. to 6 in. wide), and parquet tiles (6-in. by 6-in. blocks made up of small pieces of wood that form geometric designs).

above • This light hardwood floor, with its polished finish, reflects the kitchen's natural light, making it brighter—and cheerier—in the process. Because the floor's pale color contrasts with the cabinetry, the storage pieces become more prominent.

above • Soft woods like pine are more prone to nicks and dents but when the setting is in casual country-style rooms, it simply adds to the charm. In this living room, the pale yellow hue of the wood teams up with red furnishings to create warmth.

Dark hardwood floors are a staple in traditional interiors, with the wood species used for trim matched to the floor to create a cohesive look. The dark oak of this flooring, for instance, is echoed on the nearby stair treads and banisters.

Hardwood floors are easily damaged by water, so they have to be sealed. Most flooring available at home centers comes prefinished, but if you're installing a custom version it will need to be finished post installation with either a penetrating oil followed up with wax or a waterproof polyurethane. If properly sealed, however, hardwood flooring can be used almost anywhere in the house (with the exception of wet areas such as laundry rooms and bathrooms). If well cared for, a solid-wood floor will last the lifetime of your home. Light scratches, the result of normal wear and tear, can be buffed out; if the entire floor needs to be revived, it can be sanded and refinished.

An alternative to hardwood is engineered-wood flooring, which consists of a thin layer of wood veneer glued on top of a layer of plywood. Engineered wood is less affected by moisture, more dimensionally stable, and can be installed faster than its solid counterpart. The cost, however, is about the same as solid wood. Most engineered flooring comes in tongue-and-groove strips, which must be stapled or glued to the subfloor, although some are designed for floating installations below grade, over concrete, or anywhere the floor is relatively level. Practically all engineered flooring comes prefinished. Because these veneered types typically range from ½ in. to ¼ in., only the thickest can be fully sanded and refinished.

right · **Engineered-wood floors are appropriate for almost any room, making them a good choice for open floor plans. In this city loft, the handsome flooring underscores the living/dining area, then runs on back to the kitchen where it gets harder use.**

facing page top and bottom · **Parquetry floors—made up of mosaic-like pieces of wood to form geometric patterns—add visual interest in a subtle way. As these two kitchens illustrate, you'll find parquetry in patterns and wood species both rustic and refined.**

Keep It Green: Cork and Bamboo

Not only do cork and bamboo bring color and texture to a room but they're also environmentally friendly. Cork comes from the bark of a tree that can be harvested once every 10 years without doing any damage to the tree, while bamboo, made from an Asian grass, matures in about 6 years. Here are a few details worth noting:

Cork is typically sold in tile or sheet form and is easy to install. Because each cubic inch of cork contains millions of tiny air bubbles, it's comfortable to walk on. Plus, it feels warm underfoot, it's hypoallergenic, it deadens sound, and it acts as a thermal insulator. This material, though, does need to be sealed to protect it from moisture.

Bamboo is more like wood in terms of hardness and is most often found in either its light natural color or "caramelized," a mellow brown created when the manufacturer heats the material, caramelizing the sugars in its fibers. Like cork, bamboo needs to be sealed, typically with polyurethane.

Painted Floors

Whether you have a less-than-perfect hardwood floor or simply want to express your creativity, a painted floor can be the solution. Manufacturers offer paints that are specially formulated for floor use, but you can also use latex, as long as it's high quality. To protect your design for years to come, be sure to finish with a coat of polyurethane.

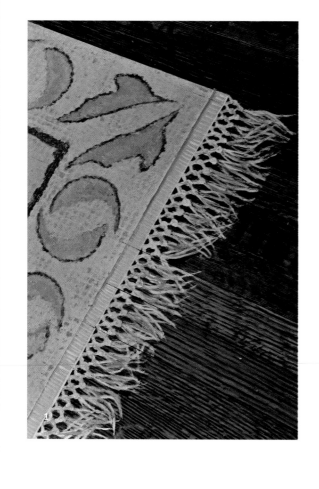

1. The fringe added to the ends of this painted-on rug is slightly askew, making you look twice to see if the floor covering is the real thing or not. 2. There's no danger of tripping on a hallway rug when it's stenciled right onto the floor. This one lightens the dark hardwood while bringing together various neutral shades in the space. 3. A true marquetry floor—with inlaid pieces of wood in various shapes, sizes, and species—can be prohibitively expensive. This stenciled approach provides the same look at a fraction of the cost. 4. Teamed up with plenty of crisp white woodwork, this green-and-yellow painted checkerboard floor gives the entry a country-fresh quality. 5. By its very nature, a parquetry floor has visual interest, given its mosaiclike pieces of wood. This one gets another layer of appeal via a stenciled pattern applied on top.

Wood flooring in this room is reserved for directly under the bed, creating the look of an area rug. The same wood covers the wall in back of the bed, then extends around to form a partial wall, wrapping the area with a blanket of warmth.

Defining Rooms with Different Floors

Today's open floor plans—even homes with expansive doorways between spaces—can blur room boundaries. One way to make a distinction, though, is with a change of flooring. Here, a hardwood floor defines a living area while tile is used in the adjacent space. To make the delineation even more clear, the tile doesn't line up parallel to the wood planks but, instead, meets them on angle.

bottom left · The medium tone of this hardwood floor is a welcome contrast to the darker hues of the traditional furniture. Pale-painted walls also do their part to keep the room from feeling weighted down.

bottom right · For water-prone areas such as the bath, recycled or reclaimed woods can typically stand up to the task. This type of flooring tends to have an inherent sense of rustic charm, making it a good fit for this country-style space.

Hard-Surface Flooring

Given that the floor is such a large expanse in a room, it's an important consideration in terms of design. But practical matters have to be weighed as well—the wear and tear the floor will have to take.

LINOLEUM

VINYL
$

- Resilient, so it's relatively soft underfoot
- Easy to install and maintain
- Comes in various colors and patterns, both sheet and tile form
- Inlaid vinyl is durable, handsome, and colorfast; lesser types can yellow or patterns can fade
- Sheet vinyl is more water-resistant (fewer seams) but vinyl tile is easier to patch

BAMBOO
$$$

- In natural form, provides a warm look; can be colored with dye-based stains
- Very durable; harder than oak
- Can be refinished numerous times
- A "green" choice, it's eco-friendly

WOOD
$$$

- Warm color and distinctive grain offer natural beauty
- Available in solid planks and strips as well as engineered types
- Solid wood expands and contracts with changes in humidity, which can leave gaps between boards
- Softwoods such as pine dent and scratch easier than hardwoods such as oak
- Can be refinished a limited number of times

TILE
$$

- Vast assortment of colors, textures, and patterns
- Highly durable
- Must be sealed to resist stains
- Hard and cold underfoot
- Must be sealed to resist stains
- Can crack if heavy items are dropped on it

STONE
$$$

- Extremely durable
- Polished stone (unlike that with a honed finish) can be slippery when wet
- Uncomfortable to stand on for long periods of time
- Requires periodic sealing against stains and moisture

LAMINATE
$$

- Wide array of colors and patterns, including stone, wood, and tile look-alikes
- Easy to install and maintain
- Durable top layer resists dents, scratches, and water damage
- Relatively soft underfoot

LINOLEUM
$$

- Natural product made from linseed oil and a mix of materials such as cork, wood, and limestone
- Available in sheet and tile forms
- Durable and comfortable underfoot
- New no-wax surfaces make it easy to maintain

CORK
$$

- A natural, sustainable material
- Extremely comfortable underfoot
- Can be purchased in plank or tile form
- Not resistant to fading or denting

CONCRETE
$$$

- Extremely durable
- Can be stained in a variety of colors
- Nonresilient; uncomfortable to stand on for long periods of time
- Must be sealed

CONCRETE

HARDWOOD

STONE

CORK

CERAMIC TILE

Tile affords a variety of practical and decorative possibilities. With this versatile material, you can infuse a room with any color, pattern, or texture you desire. At the same time, you can make a small surface appear larger or visually divide an expansive space. Ceramic tile is available either *glazed* or *unglazed*. Glazed ceramic tile is one of the most popular options. It comes in an assortment of sizes, ranging from 1-in.-sq. mosaics up to expansive 16-in. by 16-in. squares, plus all manner of border and trim. And there's no less variety when it comes to texture, from high-gloss to matte finishes, glass-smooth to highly textured surfaces.

Because all tile is not created equal, it's important to carefully consider the durability factor. Manufacturers have taken most of the guesswork out of it, having come up with a wear-rating scale for a tile's glaze. On a scale of 1 to 5 (1 being purely decorative and 5 being heavy-duty), those that rate 3 or higher are suitable for flooring applications. (Unglazed tiles have color throughout and therefore do not require a wear rating.) Equally important is the coefficient of friction (COF) rating, which indicates a tile's slip-resistance. COF ratings range from 0 to 1, with tiles 0.6 and higher considered slip-resistant. Tile in highly trafficked areas or in water-prone spots such as bathrooms should always have a rating on the high end of the scale.

As a general rule, tile is more expensive than other flooring options. And before installing this alternative, be sure that the subfloor is strong enough to support its weight.

above · When a tile floor features a prominent pattern, a border can keep it visually within its bounds. This border doesn't surround the lattice pattern on the same plane, as you would expect; instead, it's positioned at a right angle, rimming the room at baseboard level.

facing page · In this casual eating area, blue, yellow, and white tiles team up to fashion a floor covering reminiscent of a rug, given its distinct hexagonal motifs. Because the rest of the room's furnishings are primarily white with a wealth of natural light, the room can handle such a busy pattern.

Once durability and slip-resistance are addressed, ceramic tile choices come down to personal preference. Small tiles, like mosaics, provide more options in terms of creating intricate patterns. However, large tiles have their own distinct advantages. There are there fewer tiles to install, which translates to fewer grout joints to keep clean. In addition, fewer grout lines make the floor surface appear as more of a cohesive whole, often visually expanding the area in the process. On the other hand, grout can be treated as yet another decorative element. Instead of using gray, taupe, or another dark neutral hue (white and light colors aren't recommended for floor because as they show dirt from foot traffic easily), consider a tone that complements or contrasts the tile or the overall room scheme. Grout—a porous product— should always be sealed to help keep it clean and prevent cracking.

For all its assets, ceramic tile does have its downside. Although maintenance is simple and its good looks are long lasting, ceramic tile is cold underfoot unless radiant heat is installed beneath it. Tile tends to be noisy, too; there's no mistaking when someone is so much as walking across the floor in hard-soled shoes. And because tile is nonresilient, it's not the most comfortable surface to stand on for long periods of time, something to consider if you love to cook and are in the kitchen for extended stretches.

top · **Design twists can come in simple forms. In this bathroom, a tile floor in muted monochromatic tones is interspersed with coordinating smaller squares. These are placed randomly, adding an element of surprise.**

bottom · **Basic black and white tiles make up this bathroom floor, but the resulting design is anything but ordinary. The black tiles were reserved for the border, done in a Greek-key motif.**

facing page · **A little ingenuity is all it takes to create a one-of-a-kind pattern. In this mudroom, tiles in different sizes and colors combine. Because they're all in muted tones, dirty footprints are not so obvious.**

QUARRY, TERRA-COTTA, AND BRICK

Unglazed ceramic tiles, such as quarry or terra-cotta, have a matte finish. Like their glazed counterparts, they're durable; the difference is that they're porous, so they need to be sealed upon installation to prevent staining. *Quarry* consists of one color of hard-fired clay throughout the body of the tile. It's typically thought of as being a deep red color, but black, tan, and other colors are also available. Quarry tile comes in a wide range of shapes and sizes, and it's also a good choice for high-traffic areas because there is no pattern or finish to wear off.

Terra-cotta (which translates to "burnt earth") is similar to quarry tile, but its color is typically limited to the conventional dark red as well as pale pink or ochre. This particular flooring material, which measures at least ½ in. thick, can be either hand-made or machine-produced. Handmade tiles are characterized by their irregular shape and textures (it's not uncommon to see animal tracks in individual tiles where the animals walked over it during the drying process). Machine-made versions are more uniform in both color and shape (they're traditionally square), but even these can be manufactured to have an aged appearance to add character.

Brick was exclusively handmade until about the mid-19th century, its variations in color and texture all part of the charm. Today's machine-made versions are much more uniform, although hand-made varieties are still sought after, as are salvaged bricks. In addition to being sealed, brick should also be waxed.

right · **Tile with the same matte finish as brick teams up with pavers in this entry, creating a permanent rug. In this kind of application, it's important that the tiles and the pavers have the same thickness so there are no uneven surfaces to trip on.**

facing page · **This herringbone pattern, angular by nature, is a welcome change of pace in a room where the lines of the remaining furnishings are strictly horizontal or vertical.**

above · **Punctuated with light ceramic tiles, this quarry tile floor adds an important element of visual interest, given the predominance of solid-color surfaces throughout the rest of the room.**

Adding Warmth with a Brick Floor

There's no denying that a brick floor lends a certain warmth to a room. But an entire room laid out in brick means a lot of weight on the subfloor, too. This kitchen floor has it all—a lot of warmth with just a little extra weight, thanks to thin brick pavers. Pavers are not nearly as deep as traditional bricks yet they don't give up a thing in terms of style. Plus, the surface dimensions are slightly larger than their conventional counterparts, meaning fewer grout lines throughout the room and a greater concentration of the brick color. That's an advantage in this country kitchen, where the floor covering picks up the warm hues of the freestanding wood island and ochre-colored cabinetry.

above · The color of the brick flooring in this kitchen is similar to that of the cabinetry, allowing the eye to move easily from one to the other and making the room seem more spacious.

left · Brick pavers in this kitchen create a sense of rhythm, their rectangular forms repeating those found in the island and kitchen cabinetry. A brass light fixture and backsplash interrupt with rounded forms, though, to keep the space from seeming staid.

left · A pair of French fauteuil chairs, characterized by their wooden frames and open arms, take their places on opposing sides of a desk with the same heritage. The surprise element is the brick floor, which provides an informal twist that makes the area more inviting.

below · Brick floors are particularly appropriate for traditional interiors. The long stretch of brick in this entry is reminiscent of old-fashioned cobblestone streets. From a purely practical point of view, brick makes sense in a high-traffic area like this because it can take hard wear and it cleans up easily.

STONE

Another flooring option is stone tile, a category that includes granite, marble, slate, and limestone. Some varieties, such as granite, are practically indestructible, while others are vulnerable to scratching, cracking, and other wear. (Imperfections, however, may make a stone floor even more attractive.) Dimensional, or gauged, stone is cut to a uniform size and thickness and is installed much like ceramic tile. Conversely, hand-split, or cleft, stone tiles vary in size and thickness. And surface finishes are just as varied as the types of stone: They can be matte, polished, honed, antiqued, or even sandblasted. Thus, it's important to keep the end use in mind. Stone tile with a highly polished finish, for instance, may be dulled by heavy floor traffic, so you may want to limit it to areas where only soft footwear is worn such as in a master bath. Choices are becoming more diverse all the time, but some of the most popular are:

• **Granite**—The allover grainy pattern of granite—found in a wide range of colors, from grays and greens to rich yellows and reds—gives it a depth that's inherent to its appeal. This natural stone is hard-wearing, too, due in part to its low level of moisture absorption.

• **Marble**—Beyond its beautiful graining, marble has the advantage of being water-resistant, but it should still be properly sealed. Honed or matte finishes are best for floor applications since they're the most slip-resistant and hide scratches well.

• **Slate**—A deeply veined stone that's available in a wide variety of colors, slate can be split to create a truly unique textured surface. It's typically less expensive than granite, marble, or limestone but—like its counterparts—normally requires a sealer of some kind.

• **Limestone**—The purest form of limestone is white, but this stone is also found in other neutral hues including blue-gray. Paler limestone is especially porous, while harder varieties, with coarser grains, have more inherent nonslip qualities.

above • Terrazzo—a composite material that typically incorporates marble, granite, or glass chips—has a polished surface. In this dining area, its smooth quality is a welcome textural contrast to the wooden base of the table and webbed backs and seat of the chairs.

far left • The blue-and-white color scheme of this bath is no coincidence: It's inspired by the bluish veining on the white marble throughout the room. Thick slabs of the material show up on the vanity, backsplash, and tub surround, but on the floor it takes the form of thinner tiles, adding less overall weight.

left • Pieces of slate form an interesting random pattern in this sitting spot. The built-in benches, in contrast, have a more straightforward design, incorporating the floor's dark, neutral hue as an accent color and thus tying the two elements together.

above • In a space that has multiple points of entry where people are regularly passing between indoors and out, concrete is a smart flooring choice because it's tough and easy to keep clean. Concrete is not without decorative appeal, either; this example has a mottled stain, giving it extra dimension.

VINYL, LINOLEUM, AND LAMINATE

Within the resilient flooring category are vinyl, linoleum, and laminate. Characteristically softer and quieter than other hard-surfaces floorings, *vinyl* is particularly easy to maintain, making it a good choice for kitchens, bathrooms, laundry rooms, and mudrooms. Some types are available in sheet form—up to 12 ft. wide—but this flooring material comes in 12-in. and 18-in. tiles, too, lending itself to any number of patterns. Vinyl can be one of the least expensive options you'll find, but it's also susceptible to dents and gouges, which can be patched.

Linoleum was popular until the 1960s when easier-to-care-for vinyl was introduced. Today, however, linoleum is making a comeback in a big way, even though vinyl is available in more color and pattern options. Because it's porous, linoleum has to be waxed occasionally, but vinyls often need a coat of polish to retain their good looks, too. The other primary reason linoleum is on the rise: It's "green," made of natural materials (vinyl is synthetic).

Made of multiple layers bonded together for strength—such as resin, wood fiber, and kraft paper—*laminate* flooring is compacted under pressure and then transformed into planks. The surface of laminate flooring is actually a photographic image printed onto a thin, decorative layer that, in turn, is protected by a wear layer. The imagery is realistic, taking on the appearance of other materials such as wood, tile, and stone. That makes laminate a good alternative for homeowners who want the look of the real thing at a fraction of the price.

right • **Black-and-white vinyl tile invariably makes a stylish statement, especially in a checkerboard pattern. A black border around the edges, though, more clearly defines the floor as a decorative element.**

left • A laminate floor is a good choice in the kitchen; it can replicate the look of hardwood but is easier to maintain. Plus, it's more comfortable to stand on for long periods of time.

below • A gray vinyl floor in this contemporary kitchen picks up the grays of the granite counter-top, the metal bar stools, even the hood over the stove. In terms of style, today's vinyls can compete with any other hard-surface flooring.

Soft-Surface Flooring

Not only do soft floor coverings provide warmth under-foot, but also their color and pattern possibilities are all but endless. Unlike their hard-surface counterparts, they don't scratch or crack. Plus, they provide a level of soundproofing and insulation. The conventional choice in soft floor coverings has long been carpet, but there's nothing conventional about it anymore. In addition to wall-to-wall varieties, you'll also find easy-to-apply carpet tiles, which you can use to create the look of a solid-color rug or a mix-and-match effect. Meanwhile, area rugs are showing up in new forms and fibers, while natural matting such as seagrass and sisal has seen a surge in popularity, thanks to today's more casual lifestyles.

CARPET

The most common types of carpet construction are level-loop pile (loops of equal height), multilevel-loop pile (two or three different loop heights), cut pile (loops cut to create various surface finishes), and cut-and-loop pile (a combination of cut and looped yarns). A ber-ber, for instance—a good choice for a family room or a child's play space—can be level loop or multilevel. And a good example of cut pile is a plush, often the first choice for bedrooms and living rooms. Meanwhile, cut-and-loop carpets, often referred to as sculptured, have an inherent texture that not only provides visual interest but also minimizes footprints and vacuum marks.

Increasingly popular are carpet tiles. Measuring approximately 20 in. by 20 in., they come in every imaginable color and pattern. And the creative options for this install-it-yourself flooring are just as vast. You can replicate the look of solid wall-to-wall carpet, use patterned tiles to create a room-size rug, or mix things up—using a combination of solid colors and patterns—to design a one-of-a-kind floor covering.

above • Oriental-style runners are a good option for traditional hallways. Not only do they protect the most-traveled portion of the floor but they also add color and pattern to a space that typically has little room for other attention-grabbing furnishings.

above • The area rug is the undeniable star of this space. But the graphic pattern of this floor covering—not to mention its vivid colors—requires large doses of solid color to keep the scheme on an even keel.

A light wall-to-wall carpet, such as this beige version, can provide a canvas against which special furnishings can stand out. As with the walls, the light neutral provides a visual resting place for the more intense red and black pieces.

For conventional broadloom carpet, construction greatly determines how well it will hold up over time. It's important to assess a carpet's pile (the height of the yarns) and density (yarns per square inch); for the latter, the higher the number, the better. To get a quick read, perform the "grin" test: Fold a carpet sample back, forming the floor covering's "grin," to see how much of the backing is exposed. The less backing you see, the denser—and more long lasting—your carpet will be.

Carpet fibers include natural options, including wool, as well as synthetics, such as nylon. Whatever your preference, purchase the best that your budget allows, especially for high-traffic areas.

• **Wool**—A natural fiber noted for its luxurious feeling and rich look, wool is extremely soft underfoot. Although it's one of the most expensive carpet fibers, it's durable and soil resistant.

• **Nylon**—Perhaps the most popular synthetic fiber, nylon can stand up to heavy traffic and—when treated properly—resist soil and stains. While it's available in a wide range of colors and patterns, nylon is prone to static.

• **Polyester**—This synthetic fiber is stain resistant and can withstand moderate foot traffic. And, while it's less expensive than nylon, polyester carpet is prone to pilling and shedding, too.

• **Olefin**—Also known as polypropylene, olefin is both wear- and stain-resistant, making it a good choice for high-activity areas. Though not as soft as some options, it cleans easily and is affordable.

Just as important as choosing the right carpet is selecting the right pad, which provides softness and support, and extends the life of your floor covering. For most residential carpet applications, use a pad or cushion no more than 7/16 in. thick. If your carpet is a berber or some other low-profile type, choose one no more than 3/8 in. thick.

above • **The basic use-three-patterns formula works beautifully in this master bedroom. There's a large-scale motif in the bed linens and draperies, solid colors in the loveseat and walls, and a medium-scale pattern underscoring it all in the carpet.**

DETAILS THAT WORK

Adding Stair Rods

At first glance, stair rods may appear to be the "glue" that hold a stair runner in place, but in fact they're purely decorative, adding a traditional touch. Stair rods, which should measure at least 1½ in. longer than the width of your runner, come in a variety of lengths and can be custom-cut—even bent to suit curved stairways. There are many types of finials to choose from, too, including round, pineapple, and acorn shapes.

If you're considering a patterned carpet like this one, choose it before any of the other furnishings—it's easier to match fabrics and wall coverings to carpet than the other way around because carpet patterns are more limited.

right · A soft brown carpet grounds this subtle scheme, its color just as warm as the surface itself. It's a pleasing contrast for the rest of the room's neutral hues, including sage green walls that have the same go-with-anything quality.

below · Carpets with bright colors are good companions for beautifully designed furniture in neutral shades. One plays up color, the other form—two important elements in any room.

Creating Continuity between Rooms

Creating design continuity between certain spaces, perhaps between a kitchen and adjoining family room or living and dining areas, can make the two appear as one, each seeming more spacious (playing off the other's dimensions) in the process. This master bedroom and bath accomplishes that feat with a common color. A soft green covers the walls in both rooms, establishing a link even though the architecture isn't a perfect match. In the bedroom, wall paneling reaches just above mid-level, topped off by a white-painted plank. Meanwhile, walls are also wood paneled in the bath, but here they are completely covered in a horizontal fashion. The difference is subtle but just enough to make each space distinctive.

right · Space dictated that the vanity in this bathroom be directly under the windows. A suspended round mirror, though, provides the requisite grooming aid.

Soft green walls are accented with crisp white trim in this master bedroom, creating a soothing feeling. The pale backdrop is in sharp contrast to the dark wood furniture, making the latter stand out prominently.

Soft-Surface Flooring

The visual appeal of soft-surface flooring is unquestionable. But carpet and area rugs serve a practical purpose, too. They're soft underfoot and can provide both sound and thermal insulation.

CARPET
$$–$$$

- Soft and comfortable underfoot
- Available in a wide variety of colors, textures, and patterns
- Not conducive to water-prone rooms such as baths
- Stains can be difficult to remove; stain-resistant finishes can improve practicality

AREA RUGS
$–$$$

- Offered in a wide assortment of colors, patterns, and textures
- Range in size from 2 ft. by 3 ft. all the way up to room-size rugs
- Require some kind of pad to keep them from sliding (on hard-surface floors) or creeping (on soft-surface floors)

NATURAL MATTING
$–$$

- Can be used as a wall-to-wall floor covering or an area rug
- Relatively inexpensive
- Comes in limited colors and patterns
- Stains can be difficult to clean

SISAL RUG

ORIENTAL RUG

BRAIDED RUG

AREA RUG

CARPET

AREA RUGS

When shopping for area rugs, it quickly becomes obvious that most are available in standard sizes, ranging from small scatter rugs in 2-ft. by 3-ft. sizes to those that will fill an entire room, like 8 ft. by 10 ft. and even 9 ft. by 12 ft. Runners up to 12 ft. long are also available, as are rugs that are round, square, and even hexagonal in shape.

So how do you know what size you need? To a large degree, it's personal preference, but there are a few guidelines to follow, too. For instance, if you're looking for a rug that will define a conversation area, the right one will accomplish one of two things: It will either be large enough so that all of your seating pieces will fit comfortably on top of it or it will be at least large enough for the front legs of each one to fit. However, don't mix the messages; the sofa shouldn't be completely on the rug while an accompanying chair can only fit its two front feet. In the dining room, it's perfectly acceptable to put an area rug beneath your table and chairs, but make sure that it's big enough so that when a seated diner pushes back his chair, the back legs don't get caught in the process. And in the bedroom, a rug placed underneath the bed should extend far enough so there's room to step onto it from either side—and underscore bedside tables, too.

top • Shag rugs, such as this mottled gray-and-white version, are a good fit for contemporary interiors, adding texture to a space where most surfaces are slick or smooth.

bottom • This bedroom is appropriately quiet with its soft approach to a red, white, and blue scheme. But a strong splash of color, in the plaid rug, keeps it from falling asleep.

left • Taking a cue from the Oriental-style rug in the foyer, a stair runner in the same style leads the eye toward the second floor. An exact match of the two floor coverings could have bordered on boring, so the runner is slightly different in its design and a couple of shades darker.

below • A striped rug emphasizes the length of this living room, leading the eye to a sofa that tucks into a bay. The choice of a floor covering with such a strong pattern was intentional; it anchors paler pieces throughout the space.

Cotton rugs are good for the kitchen, especially in front of the sink where water spills are inevitable. Likewise, stain-resistant rugs are smart choices in the dining room where food is ever present. But if you're choosing from a purely decorative point of view, you'll find options that range from hooked and rag rugs to canvas floorcloths, felted wools, and even shag styles. Some other popular types include:

• **Aubusson**—This tapestry-style rug is flat-woven, characteristically with a large center medallion and a highly decorative border.

• **Braided**—Typically round or oval in shape (although rectangular versions are starting to show up), this rug type—with strong Colonial roots—is made of one continuous braid.

• **Oriental**—Authentic Oriental rugs are hand-knotted of wool or silk. Oriental-design rugs, which are machine-made reproductions, are less-expensive alternatives.

• **Kilim**—These wool rugs are characterized by slits in the fabric. They are, however, arranged in a stair-step pattern so as not to weaken the rug.

• **Dhurrie**—The cotton counterpart of the kilim, a dhurrie rug has similar motifs, although they are typically lighter in color.

Even the most striking rug loses some of its appeal if it constantly slips and slides. To keep an area rug in place, it's important to use the appropriate liner. One type is used between a rug and a hard surface (a hardwood floor, for instance) to keep the area rug from slipping. If you're using a rug on top of another soft surface (carpet, for example), you'll need a different type of liner to keep the area rug from "creeping."

above • There's an easy rhythm in this bedroom, created by rectangular shapes. It starts with the eye-popping red rug, moves up to the twin-size bed, and then to the windows that showcase glorious view.

Use a Rug Liner

Rugs placed on top of hard-surface floors require liners to keep them from slipping across the room. But rugs layered atop another soft floor covering, such as this sisal, require them, too. Made of a different material than liners intended for hard-surface applications, those intended for soft surfaces will keep your rugs from "creeping." Additionally, they will extend the life of both floor coverings.

above · While jewel tones prevail in Oriental-style rugs, the rugs are available in soft pastels as well. These quieter versions are particularly appropriate in bedrooms, where the mood should be subdued.

left · Rag rugs are usually considered to be country style, but that all depends on their coloration. This one, in vivid hues, adds a welcome element of pattern to contemporary living quarters.

SISAL, SEAGRASS, AND COIR

Made from renewable sources, natural matting includes sisal, seagrass, and coir among its most popular options. It has an inherent informal look, perfectly suited to today's casual lifestyles. Plus, it's durable, affordable, and even nonallergenic. In fact, natural matting has few disadvantages. It's not recommended for wet areas such as kitchens or baths, and while it disguises dust well, stains can be difficult to remove.

More than ever, natural matting isn't restricted to neutral hues, either; you'll find jet black and tomato red among the offerings. Textures are widely varied, too, including ribbed, herringbone, and basketweave patterns. (The more pronounced the pattern, though, the scratchier a matting may be—a consideration if there are children in the house just learning to crawl.) Patterns, too, are becoming more prevalent, from dramatic stripes to checkerboards.

The differences among sisal, seagrass, and coir can be subtle:

• **Sisal**—These fibers range in color from straw yellow to creamy white. Used alone, sisal can be uncomfortable on bare feet, but when natural fibers are combined with wool or nylon, the result is much softer.

• **Seagrass**—This material is popular due to its natural beauty and strength. Seagrass rugs are durable, stain-resistant, and come in warm beige tones with undertones of green.

• **Coir**—The source of coir is coconut husks, the extremely strong fibers of which create a durable but slightly coarse floor covering. Colors can vary from a bleached look to natural to subtle gray-green.

right · When selecting natural-fiber rugs for the bedroom, look for those with less of a raised pattern and more of a flat surface. It will be gentler on bare feet.

above · Checkerboard patterns are easy to achieve with individual vinyl and carpet tiles. But sisal flooring with an oversize check pattern offers more instant gratification—because it comes in one large piece, you can put in down in one fell swoop.

Natural sisal is a practical choice for an entry decked out in laid back country style. The natural theme is taken a step further here with a split-reed seating piece at the end of the hall.

FURNITURE

Selecting the right furnishings for your home requires equal parts practicality and panache. But the good news is this: With some careful consideration, you can easily have both.

Shopping Strategies

The furniture that you choose for your home should, first and foremost, serve a specific purpose. But it can also provide a starting point for your décor, inspiring an entire color palette or becoming the impetus of your own style. Maybe you've found a sofa in a floral with all of your favorite shades or a treasured Oriental-style armoire in a rich red. Pieces like these can be the foundation of a scheme that reflects your personality.

Although aesthetics play an important role in furniture selection, there's more to consider than just good looks; any given piece has to be a good fit for your home. Sofas and chairs—not to mention beds—have to be comfortable, while storage units need to have enough room around them to easily open doors and drawers. Plus, look for furnishings that suit your lifestyle. If your family tends to live casually, consider a sofa that you can sprawl out on while watching TV, one with rolled arms that are more comfortable to lay your head against than their square counterparts. On the other hand, if you entertain formally, look for a dining table that can expand to accommodate large dinner parties. If the leaves can't be stored within the table itself (an option on some models) make sure there's nearby storage space so they're always close at hand.

Last but not least, quality construction is key. When shopping for case goods—the term for cupboards and chests, pieces intended to contain or "encase" belongings—doors and drawers should glide easily. Tables and chairs should have sturdy legs. And while upholstered pieces can be a bit more difficult to evaluate, don't be shy about it: Pick up that sofa or easy chair and turn it over to examine its frame and springs.

right • A built-in banquette utilizes this corner of the kitchen efficiently. Coupled with a small table and chair, this makes a casual eating area; switch out these pieces for an occasional table—just big enough for a beverage and book—and you have a cozy reading niche.

above • A high-backed sofa like this is a good choice to visually divide an open floor plan. Because the arms of the sofa are the same height as the back, this upholstered piece wraps its occupants in warmth—both literally and figuratively.

Placing a bed between two windows invariably gives it more importance. The window treatments act as a framework of sorts, made even more dramatic when the curtains or draperies stretch from floor to ceiling.

Seating

Because all upholstered pieces are not created equal, it's important to know what to look for in terms of quality. That goes far beyond the upholstery material; you'll need to investigate the frame and filling, too.

• **Frame**—Kiln-dried hardwoods such as maple and hickory are more durable than softwoods like pine. Legs should be sturdy; ideally, they should be a continuation of the frame, not separate pieces that have been attached. Joints should either be mortise and tenon (in which one piece slides into another) or dovetail (fingerlike pieces that fit together), while springs—preferably eight-way hand-tied—should be made of tempered steel. Finally, make sure that the upholstery and padding thoroughly cover the inner springs so that you can't see or feel them.

• **Filling**—Down-and-feather cushions are undoubtedly plush but aren't always practical because they require constant plumping. As an alternative, consider those that have a core of stabilizing springs or foam. There are also cushions made of polyurethane foam; those covered with a layer of batting are preferable to those without. (The latter is not only less comfortable but also the upholstery fabric tends to shift more.) If possible, avoid cushions filled with shredded foam.

Once you've found an upholstered piece that is aesthetically pleasing and has passed all of the quality checkpoints, it's time to take it for a test drive. Sit down. Move around. Make sure that it's comfortable for you. And if you're the type of person who likes to stretch out and take a Sunday afternoon nap, be sure that you try it out in that position, too.

right • Contemporary sectionals typically have clean lines and low profiles, allowing them to take a backseat to other pieces or focal points of a room. They're a particularly good choice in spaces with strong architecture like this because they don't compete for attention.

above • The precursor to the modern-day sofa, a settee is characterized by a wooden frame. Its size, comparable to a love seat, makes it a particularly good choice for an entry, providing a place to comfortably sit and change your shoes.

above • Upholstering a sofa in a solid color allows you to better appreciate its silhouette. This one combines traditional wingback styling with modern flair, making it appropriate in any setting.

above • In this open floor plan, a pair of black sofas would have been visually too heavy, a pair of white ones too light. The compromise—one of each—is the perfect balance. Two small ottomans, as well as the throw, add just enough of the dark neutral hue to solidly ground the scheme.

top and above · Personal wardrobes are changed out from season to season. Why shouldn't your home have the same opportunity? This living room has two distinct styles—one for the warm summer months (top) and another for the winter season (above).

SOFAS, LOVE SEATS, AND SECTIONALS

A sofa, love seat, or sectional is one of the largest pieces of furniture in a room and one of the largest investments you'll make, so it's smart to choose one with classic lines and a color that you'll like for years to come.

Which one you choose largely depends on the size of your space; some rooms can accommodate two full-length sofas while others are just large enough for a single love seat. Sectionals, meanwhile, can custom-suit your needs with armless, one-arm, and corner pieces that can make up countless configurations. It all comes down to whatever scale is right for your room. Sofas typically run from 7 ft. to 8 ft. long, although you'll find apartment-size versions in slightly shorter lengths as well as custom creations up to 10 ft. Love seats, on the other hand, are intended for just two people, so they will be shorter still. Beyond length, the two of them—in addition to sectionals—have a great deal in common. Seat cushions are generally 26 in. to 30 in. deep. What's most comfortable for you directly relates to your height—short people will find their legs stretched out in front of them if the seat is too deep, while taller folks will find their knees in their chest if the depth is too narrow. You will find examples with deeper seats, but those should be reserved for informal settings, when you're more apt to curl up with your feet under you. As for back cushions, you'll find them loose, tacked on, or part of the frame itself; which you choose comes down to comfort and the look you like (see p. 149).

Before you bring your seating piece home, make sure that it fits through the front door as well as the doorway to its intended room (less of a problem for love seats and sectionals than for full-size sofas). It's a problem that you can prevent simply by carrying a steel measuring tape with you when you shop.

right · Standing in for a conventional sofa or love seat, this wood piece—with its exposed legs—creates a breezy feeling. There's no shortage of comfort, either, which is provided by a plump seat cushion and decorative pillows.

below · A small-scale love seat makes perfect sense at the foot of the bed. This one echoes the striped theme of the canopy, while its gentle curves provide equilibrium for the definitive angles of the bed's frame.

Common Sofa Styles

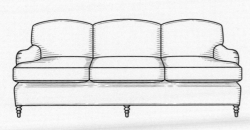

ENGLISH OR CLUB

With a slightly rounded, set-back arm, the English or club sofa is also characterized by a tight seat and low, turned legs.

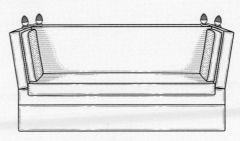

KNOLE

Inspired by a 17th-century sofa made for Knole, a house in Kent, England, this seating piece has a high, straight back and arms that can stand up straight or flare slightly, secured by cords at the back corners.

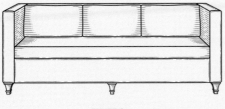

TUXEDO

Clean-lined and contemporary, a tuxedo sofa has straight or slightly flared arms that are the same height as the back.

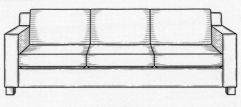

LAWSON

A Lawson sofa has square or rolled arms that reach halfway between the seat and the top of its back, which is slightly arched or straight across.

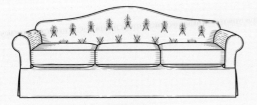

CAMELBACK

A camelback sofa, often used in formal settings, has a serpentine line that rises from the arms to a high point in the middle of the back.

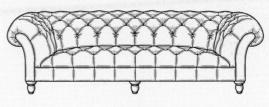

CHESTERFIELD

Easily identified by its tufted back and rolled arms, the Chesterfield is typically upholstered in leather.

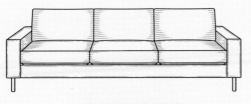

MID-CENTURY MODERN

Square lines are the hallmark of this sofa style, often seen with metal legs that are square or round.

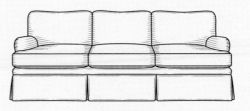

BRIDGEWATER

Similar to the club style, this sofa has low, set-back arms. Its back, though, tends to be straight across and it's typically skirted.

above • This high-ceilinged space needed seating with plenty of visual weight to keep the conversation area well grounded. A plump sectional fits the bill beautifully, aided by an oversize coffee table.

above left · A pair of sleek white sofas face off in front of this fireplace, creating a cozy sitting area. Accompanying tables are intentionally small and off to the sides so nothing impedes the flow of back-and-forth conversation.

above right · A petite sofa, with its slightly curved back, is a perfect fit against the wall in this foyer. Because it's armless, the seating piece easily blends into the backdrop—important in a space such as this where you don't want any physical or visual obstructions.

left · An L-shaped sectional like this allows you to seat more guests than a pair of conventional sofas, taking up less floor space in the process. This undisputed focal point in the room grabs even more attention with piles of decorative pillows.

UPHOLSTERED CHAIRS

At home in any room of the house, upholstered chairs have just as many shapes and styles as they do uses. Club chairs are well suited for conversation, while wingback chairs are inviting at fireside. An oversize version called a chair-and-a-half is large enough to accommodate a parent and child (or, some say, a man and a dog!). That's not to mention all of the other options, from diminutive slipper chairs—with no arms, taking up less visual space—to swivel chairs that allow you to be conversing with someone one minute and turning to watch TV the next. No matter what kind of chair you're looking for, it has to pass the comfort test. And there's only one way to conduct it: Sitting on the piece yourself.

While you can't see through a sofa's upholstered cover to examine the construction beneath, there are some quality points to check before making any purchase. Make sure that the frame is made of kiln-dried hardwood, such as maple or hickory, and that the legs aren't separate pieces but a continuation of the frame itself. Joints should be a combination of wooden dowels and metal screws and/or buttressed with corner blocks, while springs—preferably eight-way hand-tied—should be made of tempered steel. (Eight-way hand-tied springs are secured to the eight surrounding springs with heavy, knotted twine.) Finally, upholstery and padding should thoroughly cover the inner springs so that you can't see or feel them.

Like sofas, upholstered chairs are manufactured with different types of seat and back cushions. The type you choose will likely stem from how the chair will be used.

• **Loose-back** seat and back cushions are removable, making it easy to vacuum the cushions as well as the chair frame. Most are reversible, too, meaning that you can flip them from time to time for more long-term wear.

left · A gracefully skirted slipper chair provides a comfortable sitting spot in this bath. It's small enough to tuck in easily and adds much-needed pattern to the otherwise plain space.

above · This classic slipper chair features tight-back cushions, the resulting clean lines making it a perfect fit for the contemporary scheme. A decorative pillow not only dresses up the chair but also adds another layer of comfort.

• **Tight-back** cushions are an integral part of the chair frame. Although they won't shift out of place, they can look—and feel—less comfortable than loose-back versions.

• **Tack-back** cushions provide a middle ground: While they have the appearance of loose-back cushions, they're discreetly tacked to the chair's frame. The downside is that you can't remove them for cleaning, which can be cumbersome.

A pair of Bridgewater chairs, identified by their curved arms, face off in front of this media cabinet. The arrangement, with a shared ottoman, works equally well for one-on-one conversation and TV viewing. The same color as the cabinetry, the chairs don't visually protrude into the room, either.

CHAISES

The proper term for this seating piece is *chaise longue*, which, quite literally, means "long chair" in French. Originally designed for the bedroom—its length is the equivalent of a chair and ottoman put together—it provided a place to put your feet up and relax. Recently, though, the chaise has made its way into living rooms and libraries, even entry halls. And they're no longer purely traditional in design; there are just as many contemporary versions. A chaise typically has a slightly angled back, making it conducive to reclining. Plus, a small pillow can add to the comfort level while offering a decorative touch. It can just as easily be used like a conventional sofa or love seat, however; two people can easily sit side by side. Whatever the style, this seating piece is as apt to have detailing as any other type of upholstery. Some of the most common options are:

• **Channeling** is created by stitching vertical sections; it's particularly impressive on pieces with curved backs.

• **Piping or welting** is a fabric-covered cord set into the seams of frames and cushions on upholstered furniture. It can either match the piece's primary fabric or be in a contrasting color and pattern.

• **Pleats** in any number of styles can give a skirt more decorative interest. Box pleats, knife pleats, and inverted pleats (both single and double) are among the most popular options.

• **Shirring**, which is simply gathered fabric, can be used to fashion romantic skirts or to wrap the sides of a box cushion.

• **Tufting** is a series of diamond-shaped sections created by a series of buttons that are secured deeply in the upholstery fabric.

above • This chaise, with a box-quilted top and chrome legs, is a contemporary classic, but its clean lines make it equally at home in traditional and eclectic interiors.

below • Teamed with a reading lamp and a side table, this chaise—tucked into a corner of a stairway landing—provides a cozy retreat. A shirred curtain suspended from the ceiling creates a greater sense of privacy.

above · **Tufting on this two-arm chaise (you'll find them in one-arm styles, as well) gives it a distinct traditional look, which is further enhanced by the bullion fringe around the bottom of the piece.**

ACCENT CHAIRS

As their name implies, accent chairs are one-of-a-kind complements in a room. A wicker chair may pull up close to the fireplace, or a painted seating piece may sit quietly in a corner. Accent chairs add a decorative element to a room, but to make them multipurpose, choose styles that are lightweight enough to move easily—anytime and anywhere you may need them. Rocking chairs make good accents, too, and perhaps are more versatile than any of their counterparts; they're just as likely to be found in the nursery as in the living room, in the bedroom, and on the sun porch.

Accent chairs can be candidates for slipcovers, too, especially if you want to create seasonal looks. You can have a tight-fitting slipcover made to fit like a second skin or opt for one that drapes loosely. And custom slipcovers aren't your only choice. Some manufacturers give you the option of buying them at the same time you purchase your furniture (particularly upholstered pieces). Plus, there are plenty of ready-made slipcovers that can be "custom fitted" by simply adjusting an elastic or tied edge. Most are made of durable materials that can withstand repeated washings, but you'll also find slipcovers in more delicate fabrics such as handkerchief linen and organza.

While you won't find a separate section in your furniture store for accent chairs, good candidates are everywhere. A single Windsor chair may be just the thing to complete a country-style living room, while a ladder-back chair may suit more traditional needs. You may find a chair that was once part of your grandmother's dining set or a vintage model at a flea market. Even a colorful piece of wicker intended for outdoor use can be at home indoors. The options are only limited by your imagination.

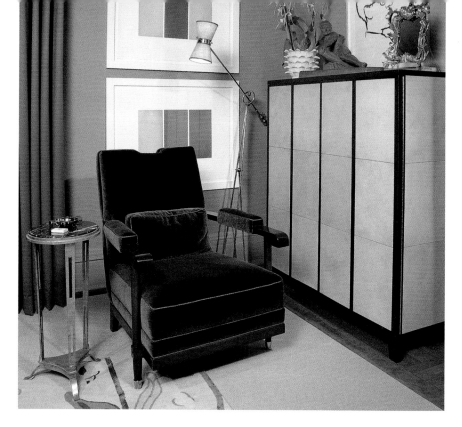

above · Looking like something that may have come out of Grandfather's library, this vintage chair—with soft mohair upholstery—has clean lines, allowing it to nestle comfortably between a contemporary table and storage piece.

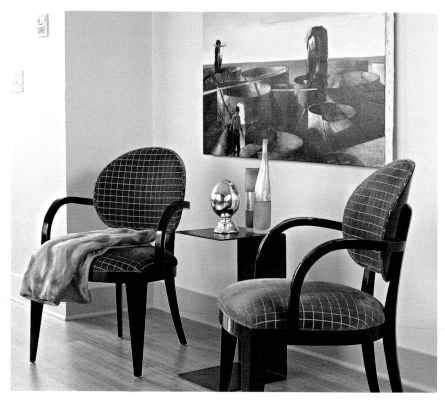

above · One accent chair is fine, but you can double the drama with two. This pair of contemporary armchairs flanks a prominent work of art, echoing some of the painting's colors to strengthen the grouping as a whole.

above • Accents chairs can take the most unexpected forms. This one originally sat in a classroom; now, it pulls up to an informal seating group, its writing arm the perfect place to set a beverage.

far left • With a chameleon-like quality, slipcovers like this give you the chance to change a chair's personality in a matter of minutes; this hot pink version adds a decidedly feminine flair to the room.

left • A side chair with distinctive lines and eye-catching upholstery, such as this French Louis XVI example, can stand in as a functional piece of "sculpture" in a front entry.

above • Around this dining table, slipcovered side chairs blend quietly into the background, allowing the host and hostess chairs to take center stage. Given their shapely forms, the brown leather chairs take on a sculptural look.

DINING CHAIRS

Today, only the most formal dining suites come with matching chairs. In the majority of instances, people are taking a more eclectic approach—finding a table they like and then chairs to go with it. And that's the key. Dining chairs can have arms or not, but they must be a good fit with the table of your choice, not only from a style point of view but also in terms of height. If the dining table has an apron—a skirtlike extension that supports the top—armchairs need to clear it and slide completely beneath. Also make sure there's enough space for people's legs (between the chair seat and the bottom of the apron); plan on approximately 9 in.

Chairs with straight backs will allow diners to sit comfortably when close to the table. It's preferable to have chairs with straight legs as well; they're less likely to get tangled up with those next to them. Traditionally, with a rectangular table, armchairs (sometimes referred to as host and hostess chairs) are placed at either end and armless chairs on each side. A circular table, on the other hand, can accommodate armchairs all around, a plus if you like to entertain—and linger over a leisurely dinner.

Finally, keep in mind that seating options aren't limited to chairs per se. In a country kitchen, for instance, a trestle table might have simple wooden benches on either side. And an increasingly popular option is a freestanding upholstered bench on at least one side of a dining table. Don't forget about built-in banquettes, either; they can slide into a sliver of space or create a booth effect, restaurant style.

top • These mid-century modern chairs pull up to a matching table, their bases providing stability. The last thing you want is for a diner to feel unsteady when leaning back in a chair.

bottom • Casual folding chairs need not be relegated to the closet. Here, their slim silhouettes—with slatted backs and seats—are just as open and airy as the dining space itself.

The Art of Dining

An all-white space gives you a blank canvas to work with, but if not decorated correctly it can leave you cold. That's not the case in this dining room, where a sea of blue solidly anchors the area, creating a soothing spot to linger over meals. To balance the abundance of white, a royal blue rug is centered on the floor, providing color contrast for the walls while letting the warm hardwood show around the room's perimeter. From there, the same shade of blue moves up to four slipcovered dining chairs, their casual look keeping the formal quarters from seeming staid. A pair of Oriental-style side chairs pulls up to the table as well, with a light and airy ambiance completely opposite that of their counterparts. It's a good thing—had all six chairs been in the slipcovered style, the look would have been too heavy.

In lieu of a chandelier, the dining area is illuminated by a more modern-looking pendant fixture. Its drum shade casts a wide pool of light, allowing diners to clearly see what they're eating—and whom they're talking to. Moving out and away from the table, the blue-and-white theme continues with a pair of porcelains at the far end of the room and then to contemporary art. It's here, perhaps, where the white walls work best of all; the artwork, all in a similar style, creates the feeling of a special gallery showing—right in your own home.

right • Floor-to-ceiling curtains in a soft, strawlike color add a hint of warmth. The color is a good choice because white window treatments would have been barely visible against the walls, making the blue used elsewhere throughout the room too strong.

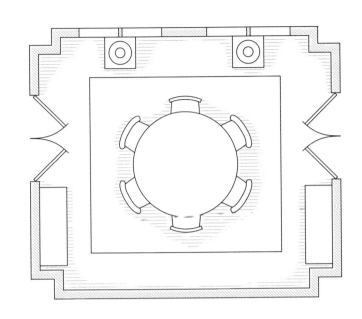

top left • A console table along one wall further emphasizes this room's Oriental influence. Two nearby contemporary artworks don't compete with it, either, enabling you to fully appreciate the intricate carvings.

left • A round dining table like this makes conversation easy, with diners equidistant from one another. The area rug is the right size, too, allowing enough room for chairs to be pushed back without getting caught at the edges.

Counter Stools

With today's casual lifestyles, many kitchens features counter seating, whether to eat a quick meal, to do nightly homework, or simply to talk to the chef. Because stool heights vary, be sure to measure the height of your counter before you go shopping. You don't want to sit so high that your knees are hitting the counter nor so low that you're practically leaning your chin on it.

4

1. Solid-color surfaces typically dominate in the kitchen, from counters and cabinetry to walls and floors. Smaller elements, such as these stools, let you have a little fun with color and pattern. 2. Like any other chair, stools with arms are more comfortable than those without. Allow a little extra space between them, though, so they're not constantly bumping into each other. 3. If you dine at the kitchen counter on a regular basis, invest in more comfortable upholstered stools. They also provide the opportunity to add color and pattern, like any other sofa or chair. 4. When choosing counter stools, let your room's style be your guide. These are just as artistic in style as the space they're in. 5. The beauty of backless stools like these is that they can slide completely under the counter, making them obscure until you're ready to call them into service.

5

BENCHES AND OTTOMANS

Small, movable, backless, and multipurpose, benches and ottomans make more sense than ever in today's interiors. It's sometimes difficult to discern one from the other, but basically a bench is rectangular and has legs, while an ottoman is typically square or round and solid all the way to the ground.

A *bench* often has an upholstered top, adding another layer of comfort. A small version might be used in lieu of a conventional coffee table or a pair could be placed at the foot of a bed. Long and narrow benches, especially, are good choices for front entries and back hallways, providing a place to sit and change shoes before going in or out. (In a mudroom, a bench upholstered in oilcloth or vinyl is easy to wipe down.) More specific in style is the fender bench, its U-shaped seat designed to wrap around the hearth of a fireplace.

Many upholstered chairs come with matching *ottomans,* but today you're more likely to see them as stand-alone elements, covered in fabrics that complement the rest of a room's scheme. They come in sizes large and small, in shapes that range from perfectly square to oversize rounds. Like benches, ottomans make perfect sense in a living room—as a stand-in for a coffee table or as a low-profile seating piece. (They're also referred to sometimes as hassocks or poufs.) Set a decorative tray on an ottoman with a tightly upholstered top, and it can be used for serving purposes. And an ottoman set on casters gives you extra flexibility, allowing it to pull up easily and join any conversation grouping.

above • Making an efficient use of space, this pair of pillow-top ottomans tuck under a Parsons-style desk when not in use. Because their black bases match the color of the desk, they blend quietly into the piece.

right • In an otherwise neutral living room, a bright red ottoman adds a surprising splash of color. While its round form visually balances the square coffee table next to it, its sculptural base is in keeping with other shapely pieces throughout the space, including an hourglass end table.

above · This bench, with its blue-and-white upholstered top, is as important to the mix of patterns in this room as any other piece. The medium-scale paisley is a good counterpoint to the more subtle stripes of the sofa and solid-color pillows.

Built-in Benches

As fitting for mudrooms as they are for living room bays, built-in benches provide the optimum opportunity to customize. They can be short or long, straight or curved, backed or backless, with storage below or not. In all cases, though, use thick enough cushions so plenty of comfort is built in, too.

1. Because this built-in is extra long, a single cushion would have slid off too easily. Instead, a series of five cushions line up, assuring more comfort for each person, too. 2. This built-in bench, a window seat, adds a pop of color and pattern to an otherwise subdued space. 3. In this back hallway, a built-in bench provides a place to sit down and change shoes or boots. A deep drawer on either side holds scarves and mittens, while an opening in the middle offers a storage spot for all kinds of everyday items. 4. The end of a hallway can be an unused space, but this built-in bench puts it to good use. The alcoved area, with a window on one side, is a great place to escape with a good book or a cup of tea. 5. Facing benches in this kitchen provide dinerlike seating in this eating area. The table is supported from the side wall, so there are no pesky legs to get in the way. Because it's supported on just one side, though, the brace has to be sturdy.

Tables

Tables come in all types of configurations—in every size, shape, color, and material you can imagine. Beyond conventional dining tables, there are end tables, lamp tables, and coffee tables, and, of course, night tables for the bedroom. And some kind of table is often desired in a front entry or back mudroom, a place to throw keys, mail, and other everyday paraphernalia. Because these areas are typically limited in space, slim console or demi-lune tables are useful options.

In a room with multiple table types, traditionalists may prefer that they all be of the same wood—oak or cherry, for instance. But an eclectic approach often better reflects a homeowner's sense of personal style. If the tables have classic lines and similar styles, you can mix and match them to your heart's content. Beyond those in general categories, there are specific table types. Some of the most common include:

- **Butler's tray table**—Originally designed for serving food and beverages, this table features a lift-off tray top. You'll find these tables in low versions, appropriate for coffee table use, or in high styles, which can stand in for a bar.

- **Drop-leaf table**—This table features a narrow center section with hinged leaves on either side, a suitable choice when you need to conserve space. With both leaves down, it can be set against a wall, serving as a console table; when dining, it can be pulled out into the room and opened to its full capacity.

- **Drum table**—With a pedestal base and a circular top, this table is named for the instrument it resembles. As a rule, it's relatively large in scale, making it suitable for the center of a foyer or a corner of the living room.

- **Parsons table**—This table has straight, square legs that are the same width as the table's front edge (2 in. to 3 in.). It's so named because designer Jean-Michel Frank taught at the Parsons School of Design, where he introduced the design.

- **Pembroke table**—An 18th-century English design, this table features short, hinged leaves on either side and a single drawer in the center. It's a good option as an end table.

above · An elegant end table takes the place of a conventional nightstand in this bedroom. A leggy style like this is an appropriate option in small spaces because it doesn't take up much space visually.

below · Built-in banquettes flank a freestanding table in this casual kitchen. It can be moved back and forth by a few inches to allow people to get in and out easily.

A two-tier coffee table like this is both fashionable and functional. The top can be reserved for treasured collectibles, while the lower level is a convenient place for reading materials, remote controls, and other everyday necessities.

above • In lieu of a traditional coffee table, this living room features a rectangular bench topped by a decorative tray that's slightly smaller. The combination creates interesting layers of texture and subtle color differences.

above • This two-tiered glass table seems to float in the space, keeping the attention focused on the colorful upholstered seating around it. Additionally, it's a good counterpoint for the boxy shelving at the back of the room.

COFFEE TABLES

The right coffee table for any room is one that's not only suitable in style but also in size. A table that's too small will look out of proportion and won't serve the surrounding seating pieces well. Each person sitting around it should be able to reach a beverage or snack easily. Look for a coffee table that's approximately two-thirds as long as the nearby sofa. That will allow everyone to access it and still provide enough space to get around the table at each end, too. If you like to keep reading materials nearby, look for one with a lower shelf that will keep them close without taking up precious tabletop space.

In terms of height, a coffee table should be about the same or slightly lower than the seats of the nearby seating pieces. (An exception is when a tea table is used as a coffee table; because it was originally designed as a place from which to serve tea, a tea table stands a few inches taller than a traditional coffee table.) The right height is important, too, if you like to lounge with your feet on the table. If that's the case, choose a coffee table with a finish that can take the extra wear, like a rustic country pine.

Although many coffee tables are rectangular, they can be found in almost any shape—round tables, solid-to-the-floor squares, even L-shapes with the two legs of the L on different levels. You'll also discover display tables, fitted with hinged glass lids for showing off collectibles in a shallow space. Alternatives to conventional coffee tables include antique trunks and blanket chests, which are appropriate for traditional or country-style rooms. They provide tabletop space and storage, too, for throws, floor pillows, and games. These also can come in handy as a place to stash extra linens if there's a sofa bed in the room.

above • The round coffee table gets its visual interest from pie-shaped sections carved into its top, giving it a retro-style edge that's unexpected—but welcome—in this eclectic living room.

above • This square coffee table not only has multiple levels, but it's also divided into four quadrants, adding an element of organization in the process. Its medium tone is a proper choice; a darker hue would have gotten lost visually against the seating pieces.

above · A two-tiered coffee table in an olive-green lacquer carries the color of the sectional through more of the living space. Its geometric forms look like modern art against the bright orange rug.

above · This coffee table is silhouetted beautifully against the much lighter hardwood floor. Plus, it's oval shape balances the more angular lines of the sofa.

above · A more formal coffee table in this sitting room could have tipped the scales toward traditional style. But a pine chest, especially in such close proximity to the grand piano, gives it a more casual, eclectic ambience.

MULTIPURPOSE PIECES

The end table beside a chair today might be at home next to your bed tomorrow. And therein lies the beauty of multipurpose tables. They can be a good fit for many places; each time they're moved, they take on new identities, practically seeming like new pieces of furniture. Some of the specific styles include the following:

Nesting tables are typically found in sets of three, their gradually decreasing sizes allowing them to fit underneath one another. They're usually set next to a sofa or chair with the largest one of the three serving as any other end table; the smaller two can be pulled out when you're having dinner in front of the TV, playing cards with the kids, or entertaining.

A slim table designed to fit against a wall, the **console** differs from its counterparts because it doesn't necessarily have four legs. In some cases, consoles have only front legs and are secured to a wall with metal brackets. These rectangular tables do, however, come in styles to suit every décor. One with smooth lines and a slick lacquer surface is appropriate for a contemporary room, while an ornately carved example is an appropriate fit for a traditional setting. Possible uses for consoles vary as much as the styles and finishes. It's common to find one in a front entry. The slim silhouette provides just enough space to drop off keys and mail while barely jutting out into the narrow hallway. In a living room, a console makes sense placed in back of a sofa; if a floor outlet is close by, a pair of lamps can be set on top.

Instead of being straight across the front, consoles can have soft curves, in which case they're called **demilune** tables. Because they have a more graceful appearance, these versions are often used in traditional interiors. Demilunes are convenient if space is at a premium—because they taper toward the back on either side, their dimensions are smaller. Demilunes, like rectangular consoles, can have four legs or just two and be secured to the wall.

above · A contemporary interpretation of a butler's tray table, this black lacquer piece has plenty of space for bedside necessities on the top level with room for a stack of to-read books on the bottom. Two levels keep things from becoming crowded.

Skirted Tables

In a room full of rectangular sofas and square-shaped chairs, a skirted round table can soften the effect. It's also at home in an entry like this, where it can add color and pattern while giving a hint of your personal style. You can dress it up in any number of ways. In this instance, a complementary topper (a square piece of fabric at least 6 in. wider than the diameter of the table) is trimmed in fringe, a contrast to the heavily corded hem of the tablecloth itself.

above • An ornately carved console table with a marble top has just enough space for a small statue, some books, and a pair of lamps that illuminate artwork directly behind them.

above • A drum table like this, with a pedestal base, provides maximum tabletop surface while taking up minimal floor space. A drawer tucked into the apron is a discreet spot to store remote controls and other small items.

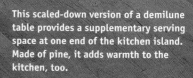

This scaled-down version of a demilune table provides a supplementary serving space at one end of the kitchen island. Made of pine, it adds warmth to the kitchen, too.

above • A diminutive table next to the tub can be sheer luxury, affording a place for favorite bath soaps, sponges, and salts, even a scented candle or two. Just be sure that the finish on the table won't be ruined by splashes of water.

left • A writing table doesn't have to be restricted to a home office. In this bedroom, it offers a quiet place to catch up on correspondence while also serving as a bedside table.

Common Leg Styles

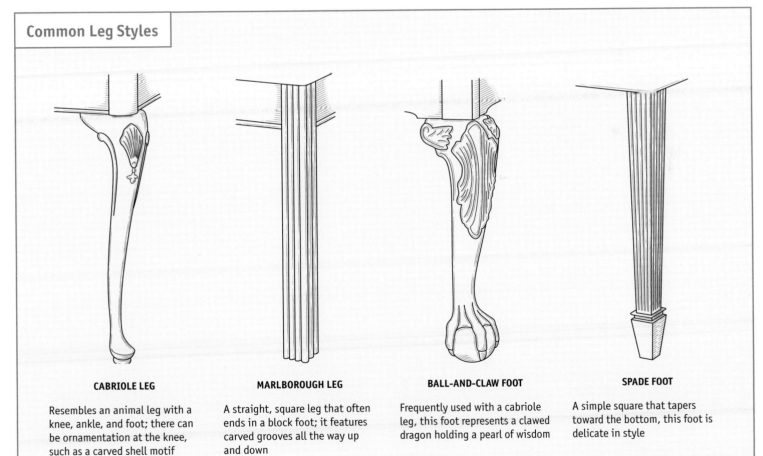

CABRIOLE LEG

Resembles an animal leg with a knee, ankle, and foot; there can be ornamentation at the knee, such as a carved shell motif

MARLBOROUGH LEG

A straight, square leg that often ends in a block foot; it features carved grooves all the way up and down

BALL-AND-CLAW FOOT

Frequently used with a cabriole leg, this foot represents a clawed dragon holding a pearl of wisdom

SPADE FOOT

A simple square that tapers toward the bottom, this foot is delicate in style

DINING TABLES

Not too long ago, the majority of dining tables were formal and rectangular, seating two people on each side as well as one on each end. Changing lifestyles, though, have vastly increased the options. Today's casual routines find people dining regularly in the kitchen or great room, with family, friends, and guests. To suit these spaces, dining tables are just as likely to be found in round or square shapes, either of which makes conversing that much easier because diners aren't so far apart and because you can see everyone without physically having to turn. All shapes can be extended, too—even those that are circular. Some transform to an oval shape with the addition of a single leaf, while others allow you to insert wedge shapes to practically double the diameter. You'll find more than one alternative when it comes to height as well. Today's casual way of life, including rooms that do double duty, has prompted dining at pub- or bistro-style tables, those that are smaller and taller than traditional dining tables. They're especially well suited for informal spaces to be used for dining or for playing games.

Shopping for any dining room table involves more than deciding on a style and shape—size is another important consideration. A traditional table should provide from 24 in. to 30 in. per person from side to side and approximately 30 in. deep (due to their casual nature, bistro tables can get by on a bit less). And if any of the dining chairs fall in front of a table leg, allow enough extra room so that the person in front of it can comfortably move to one side or the other. Of course, if you want to avoid the potential problem, simply choose a pedestal table.

right • **Mixing and matching isn't only for clothing—it also works for home fashion. This wooden table teams up with cream-colored chairs, their rush seats picking up the hue of the table while adding texture as well.**

above • A banquette tucked into a bay window is a cozy sitting spot on its own, its back a bit higher for added comfort. By adding a trestle table and a pair of chairs, it's quickly transformed into a casual dining area.

left • Had this table and chairs been set directly on top of the hardwood floor, they would have visually floated away. But an area rug anchors them, clearly defining the dining area.

right · Reminiscent of an old-fashioned kitchen when the table and chairs were set in the center of the room, this one proves the concept can be more than utilitarian. A round table, with a carved apron and base, teams up with leather-upholstered armchairs to make a high-fashion statement.

below · The warm monochromatic tones of this room—at the windows, on the walls, and in the upholstery—allow the much-darker dining table and sideboard to stand out like works of sculpture.

A built-in bench makes efficient use of a sliver of space, providing seating for a casual eating area. Although it has no back, it appears to thanks to the wood paneling that reaches high on the wall.

DESKS

Even if you're not among the ever-growing number of people who work from the home, a desk is a necessity. Perhaps it's in the kitchen for planning menus or paying bills. Maybe it's in a corner of the bedroom, a quiet place to catch up on correspondence. Whatever your needs, there's a desk—large or small—that will suit your working style.

At one end of the spectrum are slim writing tables, which can slip easily into the living room or master suite. Their petite size is no indication that they'll work less than full time; in fact, they are some of the best candidates for serving double duty as casual serving spots or bedside tables when needed. At the other extreme, oversize partners' desks that accommodate two people can be an instant focal point in a library. In between these types are kneehole desks, which typically have to-the-floor drawers on each side and an open space for your knees in the middle. And secretaries, rolltops, and drop-lid desks come with all kinds of compartments and cubbyholes, making them practical choices for those who take organization to the nth degree or as a family's "command central." Plus, with a simple flip of the lid, you can quickly conceal clutter.

The same theory applies to computer armoires—the doors open to reveal enough room for a full-size computer plus plenty of storage space. Likewise, a little-used closet in a bedroom can be outfitted with a custom workspace. If you use the space daily, the closet doors can be left off but, if not, they can be closed to conceal your work at the end of the day. For either the computer armoire or closet-turned-office, keep a comfortable—but lightweight—chair nearby, ready to pull up at a moment's notice. No matter what kind of desk you employ, though, be sure that it has at least the basics—sufficient lighting, a power source, and enough surface space on which to place a computer.

above · **This translation of a traditional kneehole desk is finished on all four sides, allowing it to be positioned facing into the room—with no unsightly bare wood to worry about.**

Study Up

A home office doesn't always require a dedicated room. If a desk is really all you need, slip it quietly into another space. This study, for example, serves primarily as comfortable living quarters. Cream-colored upholstery is striking against platinum-colored walls. Both elements are intentionally subtle, letting the window treatments grab the attention. The tricolored curtain panels, even more impressive because they fall all the way from ceiling to floor, feature a brown stripe that leads the eye right around the room. Between two of the room's windows, though, a modern desk briefly interrupts the movement. Teamed with a chair that repeats the chocolate and pale blue tones of the window treatments, the desk has a sculptural feeling—just as simple and sophisticated as the rest of the pieces in the room.

right • A dark-wood desk, matching the stripe of the curtains, would have been too expected here. This lighter version offers a slight contrast and lets you see its every detail, too.

below • Simple forms make furnishings stand out prominently in this space. There's no crowding, either, allowing you to fully appreciate each piece.

above · In its simplest form, all a desk has to have is a work surface and maybe a drawer or two. This understated version is in keeping with the straightforward approach to the room, seen in the accompanying slat-back chair and leather-wrapped daybed.

left · The slant-top desk in this bedroom keeps the clutter of paperwork at bay. The hinged writing surface drops down when it's time to work (supported by pull-out slats), then raises again to keep contents secure and out of sight.

bottom left · A secretary features a drop-down writing surface that when raised again looks like just another drawer. When this desk area is called into service, a dining chair is simply pulled over from the nearby table.

DETAILS THAT WORK

Built-in Desks

Part of the charm of a built-in desk is that it only requires a sliver of space, just enough to dash off a quick note or pay a couple of bills. They've become commonplace in the kitchen, but they're apt to show up in other rooms, too. This one, coupled with a barely-there stool, is located next to a set of sliding glass doors to take full advantage of the room's natural light.

Beds

Did you know that we spend about one-third of our lives in bed? This is why it's important to choose a good one. The first decision you must make is size, anywhere from a twin to a king. After that, choose the softness or firmness of the mattress. At least a full-size (also referred to as double or standard) is recommended for daily use by a single adult—believe it or not, a twin bed has the same width as a crib. In the guest room, a pair of twin beds offer flexibility. When needed, they can be pushed together, creating the equivalent of a king-size sleeping spot.

There are two primary factors in selecting a mattress —size and comfort. The first consideration is straightforward: Figure out what you have room for, keeping in mind that you need about 1 ft. of space on the sides and the foot so you can make the bed easily. After that, it's a matter of comfort. Most people prefer queen- or king-size beds. There are some accommodations for those who are tall. With a California king, for instance, you'll give up 4 in. to 6 in. in width but gain 4 in. in length. The most common mattress measurements are:

- **Twin**—38 in. x 75 in.
- **Extra-long twin**—38 in. x 80 in.
- **Double/standard/full**—54 in. x 75 in.
- **Queen**—60 in. x 80 in.
- **King**—76 in. to 78 in. x 80 in.
- **California king**—72 in. x 84 in.

In terms of comfort, there's only one way to find the mattress that's right for you: Lie on it. Dressed in comfortable clothing, take several models for a test drive. If you share a bed with someone, take him or her with you. Lie down in your usual sleeping position, then move around a little and even sit on the edge. If you like to read in bed, check it out in a sitting position, too. Just keep in mind that a firm mattress is not always the best mattress; it's solely a matter of what feels right to you.

above • The upholstered four-poster is the unquestionable focal point of this master bedroom, right down to its channel-quilted fabric and nail-head detailing. Its soft, neutral hue is soothing but doesn't get lost, either, thanks to a pair of blue-shaded lamps and a spring-green bench that help call attention to the sleeping spot.

far left · In this pale, neutral scheme, the dark finish of twin-size four-posters makes their intricate turnings stand out prominently. Because the bedroom is limited in space, a single nightstand serves the two sleeping spots.

left · An upholstered headboard, covered in the fabric of your choice, can add pizzazz, especially when the majority of the room's elements are solid in color. This one takes the idea a step further: Upholstered panels cover the bed's support system, including the box springs.

Sleigh beds like this one require ample space around them to showcase their graceful lines. To fully appreciate its form, a sleigh bed can even be set in the middle of a room.

FOUR-POSTERS AND CANOPIES

Steeped in tradition, four-posters and canopies have a stately quality. Their mere forms lead your eye vertically, which can make an average-height room seem taller or look right in line with a high-ceilinged space. *One word of warning, though:* Plan carefully for a four-poster or canopy; once it's through the door, you don't want to find that it's too tall or visually overwhelms the room. To get an idea of the space it will take, use newspapers to represent the size of your mattress, then put inexpensive wooden poles (found at home centers)—the same height as your bed—at the four corners. The small investment you'll make in the wooden pieces will be well worth any shopping mistakes you'll avoid.

The difference between four-poster and canopy is subtle. A *four-poster* features columns at each corner, typically tall—with or without connecting rails at the top—but occasionally not much higher than the headboard and footboard. The posts may be thin and square-shaped, as in pencil-post versions, or carved in an ornate way and topped with finials. Not all four-posters are made of wood, either; you'll also find them in wrought iron, brushed steel, and painted finishes.

Canopy beds, on the other hand, are simply four-posters with fabric added overhead. Traditional canopy beds had curtains at all four corners that could be pulled at night to keep cold air out. Today, however, canopies play a more decorative role. Some still have curtains in gauzy fabrics or colorful prints at all four corners. Others feature a flat panel of fabric over the top of the bed, edged by a short canopy about 12 in. deep. Half-canopies are a good option in small rooms, in which the canopy extends over the head of the bed only. You don't have to purchase a four-poster to get the look since the canopy and side curtains are suspended from the ceiling.

above • This beautifully turned four-poster features pineapple carvings—the sign of hospitality—on its uprights. Gauzy bed curtains soften the look while still allowing you to appreciate the detailing.

below • Decked out in pretty coral-and-white fabric, this upholstered bed lends its pattern to bed linens and draperies, too. The focal-point print even climbs the wall, suspended from the ceiling to create a canopy.

far left · This painted four-poster lends a romantic look, balancing the heavier ceiling beams. Top-of-the-bed linens are intentionally subtle, so as not to detract from the bed's delicate painted finish. Instead, pattern comes back into play in the bedskirt and area rug below.

left · A classic four-poster like this is a good choice for a child; it can be the first bed he goes to from the crib and can grow up with him right through the teen years.

Bed Linens

A well-stocked linen closet should cover the basics, including three sets of sheets for every bed in the house. That way, you can always have one set on the bed, one in the wash, and one in the closet as a backup. Two pillows per person is a good idea, too; while you're sleeping on one the other can be airing out. Other must-haves include a mattress cover, pillowcase protectors (they're easier to wash than pillows themselves), as well as one summer and one winter blanket. Beyond that, it's a matter of the decorative dressings that you prefer, from comforters and coverlets to quilts and spreads.

SHEETS
$–$$

- The higher the thread count, the softer the sheets
- The majority of today's sheets have 200 to 250 thread count; some styles go as high as 300 to 400
- Most sheets are made of cotton; those with a higher thread count are woven from extra-long-staple cotton such as Egyptian
- Sheets made of cotton/polyester blend (50/50 or 60/40) resist wrinkling but can feel stiff
- Satin sheets made of silk feel luxurious but are expensive and need to be dry-cleaned

PILLOWS
$–$$

- Feather- or down-filled are most comfortable; feather pillows offer more support, while down is softer
- Top-of-the-line feather or down pillows will last 10 years
- Synthetic-filled pillows are a good choice for people allergic to down
- Synthetics are less expensive than feather or down but don't wear as well; they need to be replaced every 2 to 4 years

MATTRESSES
$$–$$$

- Most common type is innerspring, made of spring coils covered with padding and upholstery
- The higher the number of coils, the better the bed will wear; look for 300 coils in a double, 375 in a queen, and 450 to 600 in a king
- Extra-deep mattresses can be up to 16 in. thick; make sure the sheets you buy will fit your mattress
- Pillow-top mattresses provide an extra layer of comfort; to get a similar effect, standard mattresses can be topped with feather beds
- Extra depth does not always mean more comfort; lie down and try out a mattress before buying one

Metal Beds

Brass beds are rich in tradition but popular in today's interiors, too. Over the years, the classic form has been interpreted in other metals—such as nickel—as well as more contemporary-looking silhouettes. As a result, there's a metal bed to suit any style of room.

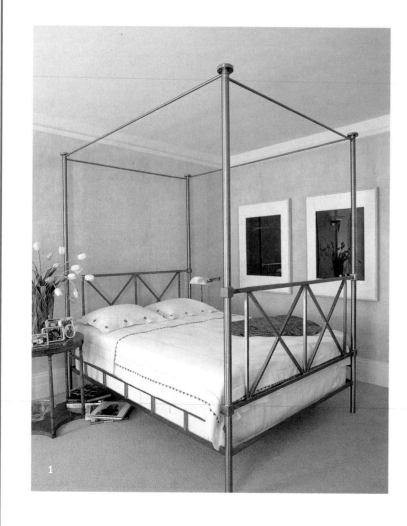

1. With a canopy, this metal four-poster would have overwhelmed this small space. Left bare, however, it takes on a sculptural quality, allowing you to fully appreciate the design of the head and foot of the bed. 2. Decorative metalwork accents this wrought-iron four-poster, becoming the focal point of this otherwise bathed-in-white bedroom. The hard surface of the metal is balanced as well by softly shirred fabric on the walls. 3. Metal beds were once all brass, but today you're just as likely to find them in shiny nickel, brushed steel, and wrought iron—even in a combination of materials, like this one. 4. Antique brass beds can be found at flea markets and estate sales as well as at conventional antique shops. If the metal is truly brass, however, you'll need to use a polish to keep it gleaming.

Making the Bedroom an All-Hours Retreat

The master bedroom has long since been a night-time-only retreat; it's now more likely to be a haven at any hour of the day. This example isn't overly spacious but still finds a way to work in all of the amenities—a restful bed, plenty of storage, plus a comfortable sitting spot. Walls cut up by windows and doors called for the bed placement to be unconventional. Instead of being tucked against a wall, it's arranged on an angle between two windows. The direction of the bed points toward the opposite corner of the room, where a petite dressing table takes its place along one wall while still leaving room for a small sitting area between it and the bed, which makes the space feel even cozier.

Armchairs are arranged for one-on-one conversation but also for easy viewing of the TV to the left of the fireplace. In fact, it's this wall that is the unquestionable focal point of the room. The fireplace itself is a few inches off the floor, making it easier to see from both the chairs and the nearby bed, while a rectangular mirror above it makes the architectural element seem more statuesque. Additionally, built-in storage to the immediate left makes the wall as a whole just as practical as it is eye-pleasing.

right · Reminiscent of a wingback chair, this headboard wraps around the head of the bed, adding an extra layer of comfort and supporting piles of decorative pillows.

facing page top · The large bed on one side of this room requires a visual anchor on the other, provided here in a practical way by a dresser topped by a tall mirror and two lamps.

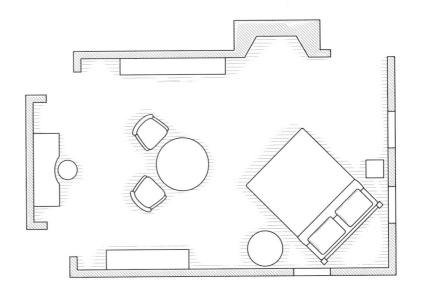

above • A fireplace is a luxury in a bedroom, and—
as this small-scale version proves—you don't need
a lot of space to accommodate one.

right · Reds, yellows, and creamy whites make up this space, carried out primarily in artwork and decorative pillows. An unexpected splash of color comes from the trundle bed, though; the bottom mattress, covered with a rich red sheet, solidly anchors the scheme.

below · The straight lines of this contemporary daybed are balanced by the more curvaceous silhouette of a side table, both standing out prominently against the darker backdrop.

above · In a bedroom that needs to accommodate three kids, a single twin and a set of bunks take up less floor space than individual sleeping spots. Here, the configuration is played up in the overall design: The artwork on the wall echoes the stair-stepped design.

above · These guest quarters are spacious enough to accommodate an entire family. Two double beds are visually connected by a wall-hung tapestry. The same warm tones reappear on the linens of the bunk beds, made even cozier by a curtained framework.

BUNK BEDS, TRUNDLES, AND DAYBEDS

Good choices for kids' rooms, where floor space is often at a premium, bunk beds and trundles make the best use of vertical space. Typically, **bunk beds** consists of twin mattresses stacked on top of one another, but in some cases, you'll find a full-size bed on the bottom and a twin on top. Or there may be a top bunk and a study or play space beneath. Bunk beds seem to hold particular appeal for small children; they love climbing up into bed, almost like an indoor tree house. That said, guardrails are necessary on the top bunk for safety's sake. It's also important that the top bed isn't too close to the ceiling; otherwise, the occupant will hit his head every time he sits up. Because the beds in top bunks can be difficult to make, choose linens that you can pull up and tuck in easily.

Trundle beds also offer two sleeping surfaces but keep them both closer to the floor. From beneath a conventional bed, usually a twin, another mattress on a wheeled base slides out. When not in use, it's completely out of sight. Be sure, however, that you allow enough floor space to be able to pull it out at a moment's notice—without having to move any furniture first. A twin-size trundle can be a practical option for a guest room or any double-duty space; set against a wall, it can be a comfortable daybed when it's not needed for overnight visitors.

Daybeds may be one of the oldest pieces of furniture on record, and they're more fitting than ever in today's interiors. A daybed can provide a sit-down spot in the foyer or provide a part-time sleeping spot in a home office. Or, it can be used to visually separate a long and narrow room, becoming a part of the conversation areas at both ends.

STORAGE

From armoires and dressers to baskets and bins, storage can do more

than serve a utilitarian purpose. Today's wealth of decorative options

often reflect a personal sense of style, too.

Define Your Needs

Some storage units have a specific purpose. China cabinets, dressers, and home entertainment centers, for instance, all have well-defined functions. The upside is that it's easy to determine how large—or small—a piece you will need. By taking inventory of your dinnerware, folded clothing, or home electronics, you can get a general idea. Just be sure to allow for a little extra room to expand in the future.

ENTERTAINMENT CENTERS

The typical entertainment center is anything but. These storage units don't come in one standard size. You'll find them large and small, short and tall. Some are so petite that they hold no more than a television set; with their doors closed, the more decorative models give nary a clue to their functional purpose. Others, meanwhile—such as expandable modular systems—have the ability to house more complex assortments of audio/video equipment. They typically include center units that accommodate conventional television sets as well as flat-screen TVs. Plus, there's ample space for stereo systems and DVD players.

On either side of the focal-point piece, matching components can be added, incorporating both open and closed storage. The complementary units house everything from toys and games to a library of books and fine collectibles, making these modular systems a particularly good choice for family or great rooms. Built-ins, made precisely to the measurements of your components, are another option. Whether you choose freestanding furniture or custom-made, entertainment centers—which can stretch to the ceiling—provide the opportunity to take the best advantage of every available inch.

A word to the wise: If a full-blown home theatre is in your future, consult with a professional first. The vast possibilities—and technicalities—of today's equipment all but necessitate the input of someone who knows the ins and outs.

above · **This custom storage unit incorporates a large flat-screen TV and four speakers as part of the design, right in step with the room's contemporary theme. For the most part, storage is enclosed, so as not to detract from the television screen.**

above · **There's no reason why modern technology can't be at home in traditional rooms, proven by the flat-screen TV that quietly blends into the background of this storage system.**

Storage is the unquestionable focal point in this family room. Accommodating everything from the TV to books and collectibles, this built-in system gets extra panache from a mouthwatering paint color and a brightly lit center section that calls special attention to favorite pieces.

The stepped design of this storage wall gives it an extra element of architectural interest. The built-in television set is a creative alternative to a flat-screen TV installed on top of a fireplace wall.

above · Low profile storage pieces are good companions for today's flat-screen TVs, especially in contemporary settings. The television can be set on top of the piece or mounted on the wall directly above it. In either case, there are plenty of doors and drawers nearby to store other electronic equipment or simply stash the remote control.

TV Guide

There are two schools of thought when it comes to TV placement: Some people prefer their TV discreetly hidden while others opt to have it out in the open, ready to use at a moment's notice. Whatever your preference, there are plenty of stylish storage solutions:

- Cabinets that look like standard storage pieces but have the ability to pop up a flat-panel TV via remote control

- Low-profile consoles on which TVs can be set; flat-panel models can be securely mounted, a bonus if there are little ones in the house

- Entertainment centers with adjustable bridges on top and base cabinets in various widths, allowing you to precisely frame a large-screen TV

However you house your set, keep in mind that the center of the screen should be at eye level when you're seated, about 36 in. to 40 in. from the floor.

left and right above · Handsome closet doors slide across one end of this bedroom, inset with green glass panels except at the top, where clear glass reveals the neutral wall color. The colored glass quietly disguises not only a flat-screen TV but also requisite clothes storage.

Housing Home Electronics

The real beauty of built-ins is that they can be tailored to specific needs. And that can be particularly important when there are small children in the house. That was the case in these contemporary living quarters; home entertainment was a must, but when not in use, the components had to be out of harm's way.

The innovative solution not only addresses the safety issue but also remains in step with the room's simple-but-sophisticated theme. To the right of the fireplace, a sliding panel moves to the top of the built-in when the family wants to watch television. There's a row of drawers directly beneath the electronics, a convenient place to keep DVDs and other related paraphernalia. When the TV's not in use, the sliding panel moves down to conceal the screen and reveal display shelves on the upper half of the unit. (For safety purposes, the panel locks securely in place in either position.) There's more storage space to the left of the fireplace, but here it takes the form of two sets of doors, each pair the same size as the sliding panel opposite, establishing a sense of balance that is comfortable to the eye.

The built-ins are intentionally light in color, to create continuity between the living quarters and the kitchen beyond. In fact, the only splash of color comes from the undisputed star—a vibrant red modular sofa that's strong enough to anchor the combined spaces.

above and facing page bottom • A sliding panel moves up and down to reveal—or conceal— a television set and other home electronics. This solution eliminated the quandary of conventional doors: how to open them wide enough so everyone can see the screen.

above · A mix of textures adds to the visual interest of this combined kitchen/family room, including stainless steel, glass tabletops, a concrete fireplace, and the wood grain of built-in storage units.

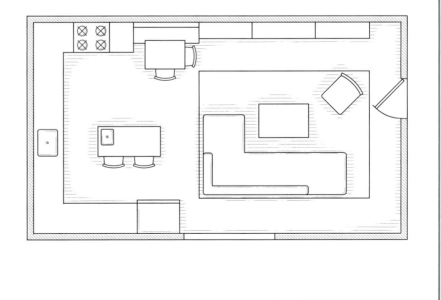

CHINA CABINETS, SERVERS, AND BUFFETS

Selecting the storage piece for the dining room is much like picking the right entertainment center—before you can make a wise choice, you need to know what will be housed within. Take inventory of your dinnerware, allowing for those pieces you still want to purchase. Be sure to include china, silverware, stemware, and serving pieces. Put table linens on the list as well as tabletop accessories such as place cards and napkin rings. Why? Keeping everything in one common place will make entertaining easier—and more enjoyable.

China cabinets are typically formal, completely enclosed with doors or drawers on the bottom and glass-fronted storage on the top. Many styles incorporate interior lighting behind the upper glass doors, highlighting treasured dinnerware and other special collectibles. Some lights are operated with inconspicuous switches, while others have special hinges that give you illumination. By simply touching the hinge you get stepped-up levels of interior light.

If your decorating tastes run toward country style, a hutch or Welsh dresser is a good option. A hutch, often made of pine, characteristically has double doors on the bottom with a combination of open shelving and closed storage on top. The top of a Welsh dresser, on the other hand, is often fully devoted to open shelves, with doors or drawers below. You can create the look of a Welsh dresser by simply positioning a wall-hung plate rack over a sideboard with a similar finish; just be sure the plate rack is close to the same width as the sideboard below. The advantage of these casual storage units is that open shelves allow you to access pieces quickly and easily. However, dinnerware and anything else stored there will collect more dust, necessitating more frequent washings.

above • Their purpose may be utilitarian, but sideboards can be equally decorative. This contemporary version is every bit as sophisticated as the rest of the room's furnishings and, at the same time, provides handsome display space.

Creative Storage Solutions

Sometimes the best storage solutions come from good old-fashioned creativity. If you prefer to keep dinnerware close at hand, opt for a storage piece with some open shelving like this hutch. On a daily basis, use the serving area for stacks of dishes—organized in plate carriers—and flatware—stashed in small vases and cups. When you want to use the area for another purpose—say, a buffet—you can move the everyday items quickly and easily.

below • The sheer size of this china cabinet makes it a strong focal point in the room. An artfully arranged collection of prints, though, draws even more attention to the storage piece.

Low-profile storage pieces in the dining room go by a variety of names, with buffets, sideboards, and huntboards being some of the most popular. They're all outfitted with doors and drawers and serve the same two-fold purpose: They safely store dining essentials and provide convenient serving areas. While buffets and sideboards are quite similar (and, in fact, the names are often used interchangeably), a huntboard can be identified by its taller height; it was originally designed for hunters, who had spent the day on horseback and preferred to stand while dining.

A huntboard typically stands on delicate legs, while buffets and sideboards can be similar in style or be solid, with doors and drawers reaching to the floor. Leggy styles take up less visual space, sometimes a consideration in a room that has a large table and chairs as well as another tall storage piece. But it's just as important to weigh the amount of storage space you need; pieces without legs offer more per vertical square inch and are sturdier, sometimes a factor for active families.

By centering a painting or mirror above it and placing matching lamps on either end, these kinds of low-profile pieces can serve as stunning focal points. What's more, many of today's models are appropriate for other rooms, too. A sideboard, for instance, can be a good fit in the family room—its storage space can be used to stash all manner of toys, games, DVDs, even photo albums. And when the occasion calls, the top can be cleared to make room for a casual buffet-style meal.

The Art of Display

Some of today's best storage units offer proof that you really can have it all: They have shelves above (behind glass doors or not), where you can display an array of collectibles, and abundant closed storage below. What's more, these pieces are typically generous in size, making them immediate focal points, too.

1. If shelves are adjustable, as in this traditional piece, vary the heights so you can show your collectibles to the best advantage and they—more than the piece itself—become the focal point. **2.** If a single storage piece is good why wouldn't one that's double the width be better, especially if you have the space and an extensive collection like this array of blue and white? **3.** This Adirondack-style hutch is ideal for a casual space but can look dressier or completely laid back depending on the contents within. **4.** With its red chinoiserie finish, this Oriental-style cabinet adds a much-needed splash of color to an otherwise neutral room. Highly decorative furnishings like this should be used sparingly to make the most dramatic impact; one piece is often all it takes. **5.** A towering storage unit is perfectly suited for this living room, given its vaulted ceiling. The piece even handles a collection of antique valises, prominently displayed on top.

DRESSERS AND NIGHTSTANDS

Bedroom storage is specific, designed to satisfy needs unique to that space. Triple dressers have traditionally been a given. With three small drawers along the top tier and larger drawers on the bottom two, they provide a good his-and-hers solution. And the accompanying mirror is more than merely practical; spanning the width of the chest below, its reflective qualities can seemingly expand a space and bounce more light into a dim room. There are, however, other creative solutions that provide the same amount of storage space. A pair of matching bachelor's chests, for instance, can be placed side by side and then visually connected with a mirror centered over them. Or each can be topped with its own individual mirror—round ones provide a pleasing contrast to the more linear storage units, while tall, narrow versions create a greater sense of overall height. Another benefit is that this option offers great flexibility, as both the bachelor's chests and the mirrors can be used elsewhere in the house at a later date.

Like triple dressers, conventional nightstands have long been the most common bedside option. Standard two-drawer models have enough tabletop space for all the necessities—a bedside lamp, an alarm clock, and a book or treasured photo. But creativity has overtaken this category, too. Small dressers can serve at bedside, too, as can small-scale desks and all kinds of occasional tables. There's really just one rule of thumb: The top of the table or chest should be no more than 2 in. higher or lower than the top of the bed, allowing you to reach anything easily.

right • A lighthearted dresser establishes a playful mood in this room, painted to appeal to children of either gender. A matching hutch displays toys and books but keeps them safely out of a toddler's reach, too.

above • This two-drawer nightstand has simple lines, but they're well defined by intricate marquetry trim. For an added dash of decorative flair, a tassel hangs from the lower drawer pull, echoing the room's predominant red hue.

In a room where creamy white colors keep things sedate, a dark-wood dresser is a standout. It provides a visual anchor, keeping the rest of the light and airy furnishings from seemingly floating away.

Multipurpose Pieces

Beyond their decorative appeal, the beauty of multipurpose pieces is that they can move from one room to another as your needs evolve and change. The two-tiered end table that's chairside in the living room today might show up bedside tomorrow. By the same token, an armoire that houses home entertainment equipment in the family room might eventually move to a home office, providing stylish storage for supplies. Multipurpose storage pieces have the kind of flexibility that makes them—dollar for dollar—some of the best buys you'll find.

CHESTS

By strict definition, all chests have one thing in common: They're storage pieces fitted with drawers. Beyond that, the differences can be dramatic. Some chests are diminutive, with just a couple of drawers—the right height to pull a chair up to. Others are more statuesque; a traditional highboy can be a focal point in its own right, whether it's used for clothing in the bedroom or for linens and flatware in the dining room. And furniture is finding its way into the kitchen and bath more than ever before. In the master bath, a medium-size chest might be fitted with a sink to create a good-looking vanity. Likewise, a smaller one in the kitchen can be transformed into a snack station or minibar, tucked into a corner somewhere.

The most versatile chests are simple and understated, allowing them to meld easily into traditional, country, or contemporary schemes. This kind of straightforward styling has another advantage as well. Once you've grown tired of the finish, or it starts to show wear, a fresh coat of paint—perhaps embellished with stenciled motifs—can give any piece a new lease on life.

above • The mirrored finish of this bedside chest gives it a little extra sparkle, bouncing light back into the room. This is a good choice for small spaces, too; like a conventional mirror, it can visually double an area's dimensions.

above • A traditional chest in this living room provides valuable storage space. With the addition of a pair of hefty table lamps, it also helps light up what could have been a dark corner of the room while commanding presence.

above · This two-drawer chest works as well here, next to a living room chair, as it would at bedside or in the entry. Its flexibility is further enhanced by the finish; the highly decorative drawer fronts are balanced by more casual bamboo trim, making the piece equally at home in formal and informal interiors.

ARMOIRES

Centuries after they came into use in medieval times to store suits of armor, armoires can be found in virtually every room of the modern-day house. In the kitchen, they can stand in as a pantry, while in the dining room, they provide a convenient place for serving pieces. In fact, there's nowhere that an armoire can't offer supplemental storage. One of the reasons they're so versatile is because they come in a variety of sizes. While many are wide and massive, much like the original designs, just as many are narrow and scaled down for today's smaller spaces. And there's plenty of variation in height, too; armoires range from those that are no more than 5 ft. high— just large enough for a television set and DVD player—to those that stretch a full 8 ft., perfectly suited to rooms with soaring cathedral ceilings. Last but not least, they come in styles for every decorative preference, from traditional types that are intricately carved to country antiques with the added "character" of peeling paint.

Depending on how you plan to use your armoire, you can keep the doors closed on a regular basis or thrown open wide at all times. The former is a better option if the armoire houses electronics; you'll keep dust to a minimum if you only open them when the equipment is in use. An armoire used for this purpose needs to be well ventilated so the inevitable heat from the electronics can dissipate. For the best viewing, look for models with doors that swing out and slide back into the cabinet itself.

If, on the other hand, the armoire is a display space for collectibles, keep the doors open so you can fully appreciate your treasures. The shelves within aren't the only display options, either. Armoires that have doors with straight-edged tops can be used to display colorful throws or quilts.

above • The decorative painting on this armoire is characteristic of Scandinavian country pieces. Its oversize dimensions make it a particularly good choice in bedrooms without sufficient closet space, standing in as a handsome—and portable—wardrobe.

above · With its doors thrown open wide, this armoire reveals an entire library of books, just as colorful as the cabinet's painted finish. Part of the beauty of armoires is that their shelves can be configured to suit your personal needs.

top left · Set on casters, this armoire can easily be moved from one room to another. The simple styling, too, gives it a chameleon-like quality, able to blend into many different schemes.

left · A scaled-down armoire stands at one end of this dining room, a good fit for today's smaller spaces. Only the hardware reveals its Oriental influence, taking this space out of the contemporary category and making it more eclectic.

A handsome black shelf unit underscores a wall-mounted television in this bedroom. There's enough surface space on the top shelf to accommodate a pair of lamps, which makes the TV seem more like a piece of art than electronics.

above · An étagère in this living area is appropriately placed in the midst of an art grouping. On either side, the pieces are two-dimensional but, the artistic treasures displayed on these shelves are three-dimensional, giving the room more visual interest.

below · Just outside the bathroom, an open shelf unit makes it easy to grab thick, thirsty towels on the way in. A similar storage piece stands at the far end of the room, keeping other bath necessities close at hand.

SHELF UNITS

There's nothing quite so accommodating as a simple shelf unit. This is storage in its most basic form, ready to serve a purely functional purpose or support more decorative endeavors. Some pieces might sit discreetly in a corner of a room; small versions, for instance, could hold towels in the bathroom or be devoted to a treasured collection of books. Taller ones, with their extended vertical reach, might hold countless collectibles or provide a place to store fine wines (but if this is the case, a specific rack designed to hold wine should be called into service). Pieces that are open from front to back make storage easily accessible from either side, but those with solid backs—just as finely finished on the back as on the front—can be good room dividers. That can be particularly appealing for those living in loft-style spaces.

Shelf units are becoming more versatile than ever, with some now available with wheels. This makes them easy to move from one place to another, whether it's across the room or to another one entirely. Be sure that your rolling storage unit has wheel locks so it doesn't get away when you least expect it. For the same reason, make sure the items within don't get top heavy. Look for models that have raised edges so the contents don't slide off when you're on the move, either.

Finally, don't forget about wall-hung shelving options. Plate racks—three- or four-tiered units just deep enough to display a plate—are one of the most common options, but there are all kinds of other alternatives. Easy-to-install wall ledges, which look like deep, elaborate pieces of molding, can hold all kinds of small collectibles—use one alone or stair-step several. Or simple wooden shelves, supported by adjustable brackets, can reach all the way to the ceiling. This can be a good way to accommodate a growing library of books. Just be sure to keep the shelves on the short side so they don't get weighed down by your volumes.

above · Because it's set on casters, this two-tiered trolley—serving as a bar—can be moved whenever and wherever it's needed. On a daily basis, though, its mirrored surfaces add sparkle to this end of the dining room.

right · A ladderlike storage piece in this bathroom, with a single shelf at the bottom, keeps towels and washcloths conveniently close while adding color and dimension to the far wall.

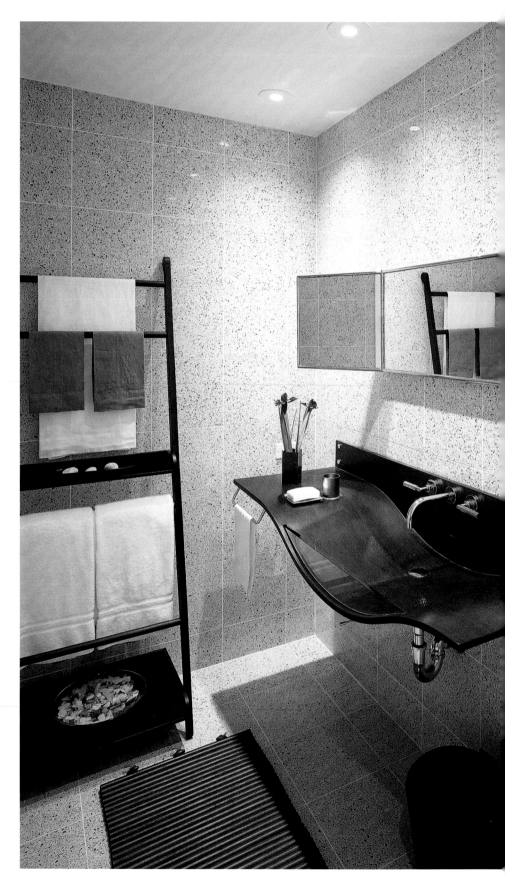

Keeping Storage Out of Sight

Let's face it: Some storage just needs to be serviceable, not prominently displayed in a room. That's the case here. Tucked between a kitchen and laundry room are two slivers of space, just the right size for sturdy industrial-style shelves. One set accommodates pantry items, while the other holds small kitchen appliances. Both, however, can be completely concealed from the kitchen via a barn-style door. This closure not only adds a bright splash of color, but it's also a space-saver because this type of door doesn't require any space to swing open one way or the other. What's more, on laundry day—by simply rolling it shut—nobody need be the wiser that stacks of clothes are awaiting attention.

A barn-style door conceals two freestanding storage units in opposite niches as well as the laundry room beyond.

Freestanding Storage

Portable storage units are some of the best buys you'll find. These hardworking furnishings can move from room to room, wherever they're needed most. From armoires to étagères, bachelor's chests to highboys, their potential uses are only limited by your imagination. By simply repurposing a piece, you can give a room an entirely new look.

1. This petite shelf unit tucks in neatly next to the shower, keeping fresh towels conveniently close. The same piece could serve as a drop-off spot for mail in the entry or hold treasured photos in the family room. 2. Antique iceboxes may no longer serve their original purpose, but they're still just as practical. Set in the entry, this one can house hats, gloves, mittens, even umbrellas. 3. This chest is the perfect bedside companion. There's plenty of surface space for a lamp, alarm clock, and book, plus drawers below for more personal treasures. 4. A traditional Chinese tonsu chest is right at home with a roomful of contemporary furniture, thanks to its clean lines and understated styling.

Built-ins

Built-in storage may not afford the luxury of moving with you from place to place, but that's balanced by the fact that it can utilize every inch of potential storage space. Don't be intimidated by thinking that built-ins have to be a colossal project. While an entire wall of custom doors, drawers, and shelves can be the ultimate luxury, even the smallest improvement can make a big difference. A window seat, for instance, can provide the perfect place for blankets, while a previously unused space under the stairway can be carved out to accommodate shelves for books. A built-in can even be something as simple as a plate rail installed near the ceiling level, ready to display a collection of transferware or Lionel trains—keeping them out of harm's way at the same time, too.

The real beauty of built-ins is that they can be custom-tailored to your specific needs using stock, semicustom, or custom cabinetry. As a general rule, cabinetry is open at eye level and closed below, so that decorative objects are stored on the visible shelves—behind glass or not—and more utilitarian items are stashed behind doors or in drawers below. Any project that includes built-ins should be carefully thought through before beginning. If you're planning anything on a major scale, though, you'll need the assistance of a professional—a contractor and perhaps a designer, too—to carry out the master plan. The overall price may end up a bit higher than if you were to go with an off-the-shelf piece, but the end reward will be greater, too.

top • In this master bedroom, the back side of a fireplace resulted in a wall protrusion. By adding built-in storage on either side, it's now an inherent part of the overall design—even a prominent place to display art.

bottom • A two-tiered table is beautifully transformed into a double vanity in this master bath. The necessary pipes are tucked close to the wall, leaving plenty of room for towels and toiletries on the lower shelf.

Cabinetry

When shopping for cabinetry to create one-of-a-kind storage, keep in mind that there are three types to choose from: stock, semicustom, and custom. The terms don't indicate different levels of quality; each group has both high- and low-end options. What's most important is that you purchase the best you can afford—whatever type you opt for.

STOCK
$

- Readily available; typically takes 1 to 3 weeks to receive
- Installation is usually a do-it-yourself project
- Selection of styles, finishes, and accessories is limited
- Because it comes in standard sizes only, filler strips (to cover gaps) may be required

SEMICUSTOM
$$

- Offers more design flexibility than stock options
- Comes in a good selection of styles, finishes, and accessories
- Can customize some height and depth
- Typically takes 6 to 8 weeks to receive
- Like stock cabinetry, may require filler strips in some instances

CUSTOM
$$$

- Comes in an almost unlimited variety of styles, finishes, and accessories
- Can be detailed with architectural elements
- Can be designed to tailor-fit storage needs
- Cost is approximately 25 percent more than semicustom
- Requires from 8 to 16 weeks for delivery

Taking advantage of every vertical inch, this built-in wall unit wraps around windows, framing the spectacular view. Built-in seating is also part of the design, making the most efficient use of floor space, too.

LIVING AND DINING ROOMS

Primary living areas—living, family, and dining rooms—are more multipurpose than ever before. In turn, they have to accommodate a wider variety of needs. A formal living room may need display space for fine collectibles but might also call for a built-in bar with space for glasses, stemware, and other serving accessories. The family room inevitably needs some sort of entertainment center to house home electronics, but a young family will likely also put a high priority on concealed storage for toys and games. And a dining room, beyond the requisite storage for all manner of dinnerware, may also need a writing table that can function as a home office on a day-to-day basis but convert to a serving area when the occasion calls.

Besides filling specific needs, built-in storage can add architectural interest. Plus, it can make a room work more efficiently than you ever imagined. A long and narrow room, for instance, might be divided by a floor-to-ceiling structure in the center of the room; a 6-ft.-long unit centered in a 12-ft.-wide space will allow 3-ft.-wide passageways on either side. And if it's deep enough, the unit can provide storage space on both sides, benefiting each end of the room. Built-in storage needn't be elaborate, though, to serve the purpose at hand and be eye-appealing. Sometimes all it takes is floor-to-ceiling shelves of books—filled with colorful volumes—to satisfy both.

top · Built-in storage on either side of this fireplace is just as straightforward as the architectural element. With a dark neutral finish—a complete contrast to that of the fireplace—the built-ins stand out, their simple square forms a good fit for the room's equally understated furnishings.

bottom · This custom piece in the dining room features glass-fronted doors, behind which stemware can be displayed, and ample closed storage for all other entertaining needs. The upper doors were intentionally designed to be high so the surface below can be used to fullest advantage—from storing items on a daily basis to serving a meal buffet style.

above • Built-in bookshelves, with enclosed storage at the bottom, are a smart solution for any living area. Because the backs of the shelves are painted a rich red, this unit becomes an integral part of the room's color scheme.

above · Floor-to-ceiling shelves turn what could have been an unused space at the end of a hall into a hardworking area. The symmetrical boxlike design has an organized look on its own, making the contents within look so, too.

right · In this dining room, a built-in china cabinet takes its design cue from the nearby windows. The glass-fronted doors of the storage piece replicate the look of divided-light windows; lit from within, the interior even has a sunshine-like glow.

Cabinet Materials

The materials you choose for built-in cabinetry should be just as durable as they are aesthetically appealing. As long as a particular material suits your sense of style and will stand up to its intended use, it's a good choice for you.

MEDIUM-DENSITY FIBERBOARD (MDF)
$

- Strong material; takes paint well
- Unlike wood, can have an unnatural appearance
- May give off volatile organic compounds (VOCs)

LAMINATE
$

- Comes in a variety of colors, patterns, and textures
- Easy to clean
- Difficult to repair chips and scratches

SOLID WOOD
$$

- Can be stained or clear-finished to allow the natural wood tone to shine through
- Available in a variety of species, including oak, maple, pine, and cherry
- Easy to repair

GLASS DOORS
$$–$$$

- Available in a variety of colors and textures
- Glass panels sometimes rattle when doors are opened or closed

SOLID WOOD

GLASS DOORS

KITCHENS

In the kitchen, perhaps more than anywhere else, it's imperative for items to have a designated "home." Unless storage space is well thought out, this room can be the most likely source of clutter. Take stock of your cooking habits and your personal style, and then come up with the right combination of wall and base cabinetry plus assorted shelves. Think beyond the conventional configuration of wall cabinets over base models, and standard drawers over doors. And if your lifestyle would benefit more from a large amount of open shelving—to display dinnerware restaurant-style or to accommodate a collection of cookbooks—plan space accordingly.

When shopping for cabinetry, you'll find two basic options: face-frame and faceless cabinets. *Face-frame* cabinets have a solid-wood frame that's attached to the case, and doors either overlay the frame or are inset flush. This type of cabinetry typically has exposed hinges; they're not adjustable and are visible when the door is closed. Some models do, however, come with concealed, adjustable hinges. Face-frames reduce the size of a cabinet's opening but, at the same time, strengthen the cabinet. *Faceless* styles get their strength from thicker cases, requiring no supportive face frame. Their adjustable hinges are concealed when the door is closed, making the inside of the cabinet completely accessible when the door is open. Because the doors and drawers almost touch, frameless cabinets have long been associated with contemporary style. Today, though, you're likely to find them with traditional styling, too, complete with panels and molding.

There are a few simple guidelines to keep in mind when incorporating shelves in any kitchen cabinet. Allow a minimum of 8 in. if you're storing cookbooks, and 12 in. to 15 in. for dinnerware. Pots and pans require deeper shelving, usually 18 in. or more. Don't be tempted to space shelves too far apart, either; it will be too easy to stack things too high.

above • Kitchen cabinetry most often has solid doors to conceal the stacks of cookware within. This built-in piece takes the opposite approach—glass-fronted doors make it easy to see at a glance exactly what you're looking for.

Under-Counter Storage

If you like to entertain and typically make multiple trips from the kitchen to the dining room, here's a way to save yourself some steps: Reserve room under the counter for a rolling cart that can deliver dinnerware to the table, then to the dishwasher afterward. (Industrial styles work well; you can easily see their contents and they move across hard-surface floors easily.) If there's enough space, designate a second cart for often-used items such as melamine mixing bowls and small appliances.

bottom left · One end of this kitchen cabinet has been converted into a wine storage spot, keeping the bottles out of harm's way but easy to grab at a moment's notice. The circular compartments are almost artistic and are in keeping with the room's modern design.

bottom right · Just inside the back entry, this storage unit offers a place for collectibles on its upper shelves and drawers below for everything from hats and gloves to kitchen linens. Alternatively, the entire piece could serve as a pantry, with small—and most-used—items reserved for the upper shelves.

HOME OFFICES

Perhaps you have the luxury of an entire room devoted to a home office. Or maybe you're content with a corner somewhere in the house. Whatever your circumstances, a well-organized office space can work just as hard as you need it to.

One of today's most popular options is a home office incorporated into the kitchen. But don't plan for a work surface and a couple of drawers, and then call it good. Think about how it will really be used. Will the space serve as a place to review recipes and plan meals? Pay household bills on a weekly basis? Where the kids can do their homework after school? If it serves more than one purpose, make sure that each is accommodated. Instead of standard wall cabinets above, for instance, consider open cubbies for individual family members or tasks. Or, if you prefer to hide papers and projects, configure an area with a drop-lid work surface (a great idea to use anywhere in the house).

A room fully devoted to home-office work can be built out with storage to the nth degree. If you want to keep a lid on the budget, though—and keep your options open for using the room for a different purpose in the future—there are other ways to satisfy storage needs. In a bedroom-turned-office, for instance, a closet can be outfitted to suit specific wishes. Remove the closet doors as well as the standard clothes rod, then take your dimensions and list of supplies that need to be stored to a local closet-planning specialist. You can have the new system installed by the pros or, many times, do it yourself.

top · **This home office takes care of the basics in a simple but sophisticated way. A desk in one corner of the room (it might be built in like this or a freestanding piece) teams up with wall-hung shelves that are just as suitable for office supplies as they are for fine collectibles.**

bottom · **A dedicated home office isn't required to have a smart-looking workspace. When it's time to do bookwork, a chair can be pulled up to this drop-lid desk, part of a dining room storage wall. When not in use, the writing surface flips up and quietly blends into the built-in.**

From a visual point of view, solid-wood doors would have been too heavy on this built-in storage wall; the home office already has a massive amount of the natural material. Shoji-style doors, with their white paper insets, lighten the overall effect.

BEDROOMS AND BATHS

As master suites become sought after as the ultimate retreat, more time than ever is being spent there. Even kids' rooms are being configured in a suite style as are many guest quarters. More activities, it seems, are taking place in these spaces, too. Bathrooms are less utilitarian and more personal spas. And bedrooms have become inviting refuges for reading, watching TV, and even catching up on personal correspondence.

Even an average-size bedroom can be configured to accommodate multiple activities, with designated storage space for each. Float a bed in the middle of the room, for instance. At the head of the bed, a custom storage piece might incorporate bedside tables on the front (as well as built-in reading lamps) and a bank of drawers for clothing on the back. Meanwhile, at the foot of the bed, a matching piece might conceal a TV set; fitted with the right mechanics, it can raise and lower at the touch of a remote control. This center-of-the-room arrangement frees up the perimeter of the room, leaving room for reading chairs and accompanying tables, as well as writing desks and any other needs. Or take a more conventional all-in-one approach and designate an entire wall for built-in storage, much like you would in the family room.

Bathrooms, meanwhile, call for built-in storage ranging from simple hooks and pegs to vanities and luxurious linen closets. But it's important to sort out what items absolutely need to be close at hand and which ones will be just as convenient down the hall. Think, too, about how family members use the room and how even the smallest built-in might enhance the space. Maybe it's a niche next to the tub that can keep shampoo and bubble bath close at hand. Or perhaps you have the luxury of an extra-long vanity; if so, borrow some space from one end and build glass-fronted cabinetry that goes to the ceiling. You can fill it with towels and all kinds of toiletries—and never wonder where anything is again.

above • At the end of this vanity, a few extra inches of storage space are all it takes to keep rolled-up towels close at hand. Because the top of the piece is higher than the adjacent vanity top, there's an extra element of architectural interest, too.

above • Custom-crafted to wrap around a bed, this built-in not only provides storage space but also incorporates a pair of nightstands. The open space behind the sleeping spot lets you see the rich wall color; framed by the storage piece, it takes on the look of a headboard.

above • Wall-hung cabinetry handles the bulk of enclosed storage in this master bath, while twin vertical units at either end of the vanity also include open shelves. The vertical lines draw the eye from floor to ceiling and back again, balancing the space by putting the emphasis less on the length of the room and more on its height.

Just for Kids

Storage for kids requires special consideration. It has to be easily accessible but have no sharp corners that might cause injury. Likewise, doors and drawers shouldn't be capable of slamming shut on small fingers. Once the safety points are covered, though, the fun can begin. Nowhere else can your imagination run as wild as with storage that's created for kids only.

1. A combination play space/loft bed becomes an adventure in storage, too. Niches are cut out in various places, making it just as much fun to put toys away as it is to retrieve them. **2.** Stair-stepped storage in this playroom includes plenty of open cubbies that can be organized by content or assigned to individuals. Easy-to-access enclosed storage below provides a great place to stash toys and games.

above · A built-in daybed works just as well for lounging as it does for accommodating overnight guests. Drawers below can stash any number of things, from toys and games to extra bed linens, even out-of-season clothing.

above · The best closets, like this one, have an abundance of both open and closed storage. Better still, they have windows that allow you to see the true colors of whatever ensemble you're assembling.

above · There's hidden storage to be found in a non-load-bearing wall, so create a narrow set of shelves between a pair of studs. The beauty of these white-painted versions lies in their contrast against the natural wood grain backing.

LIGHTING

A well-lit room is one with layers of ambient, task, and accent lighting.

Think of the three types as decorative building blocks,

each supporting one another beautifully.

Creating a Balanced Lighting Scheme

Like so many other aspects of a well-designed room, lighting relies on good balance. Ambient, task, and accent lighting are all equally important. The key is in knowing how much to use of each type—and where to use it. In a living room, for instance, an elegant chandelier might provide overall ambient lighting, while a table lamp here and a floor lamp there illuminates specific tasks such as reading. And well-placed picture lights might accent your most treasured works of art. With the right mix, this three-pronged approach can provide visual excitement, too. Given a variety of lamps at eye level, picture lights just a bit higher, and ceiling fixtures overhead, a well-balanced lighting plan creates light and dark areas that spotlight some items and leave others subtly in the shadows.

If you have the luxury of starting from scratch—adding on or building a new home, for instance—put together your lighting plan early on so that wiring can be run for ceiling and wall fixtures. Position outlets close to their respective fixtures and switches grouped close to doorways. (If your room has a complex lighting plan, you may even want to hire a lighting designer.) At all times, keep in mind what time of day you will use the room most. Formal living and dining rooms, for example, are primarily used during the evening hours, so you'll want to turn up the wattage to keep guests from sitting in the dark. Conversely, you'll want to keep the kitchen well lit so that you can clearly see the task at hand, whether it's reading a recipe, chopping up vegetables, or carefully watching something on the stove. And a family room needs hardworking general and task lighting—it's used all hours of the day and in various ways by all members of the family.

left · Looking like an assemblage of cut-glass prisms, this wall sconce not only provides accent lighting but also throws texture into the mix. Positioned in close proximity to the mirror next to it, the light it casts bounces back and forth, multiplying the effect in the process.

below · In this living room, niches reserved for treasured collectibles are individually lit; each has its own built-in downlight, showcasing the object within. The effect is impressive during the day but even more so at night, when the area becomes a stunning focal point.

Why reserve chandeliers for the living or dining room? Here, a large, ornate fixture adds romance to the bedroom. Task lighting has been taken care of with bedside lamps that have banded shades reminiscent of the tailored bed linens.

Ambient Lighting

In simple terms, ambient (or general) lighting allows someone to walk safely through a room—to keep from stepping on a toy or running into the furniture. Additionally, though, ambient lighting gives a room a soft, overall glow. Some of the most common ceiling fixtures in this category include chandeliers and pendant lamps. A crystal chandelier is befitting in a traditional living room and its prisms are more than merely decorative—they reflect light right back into the room, adding a sparkling touch in the process. Meanwhile, pendant lamps might be more appropriate for a contemporary setting, whether it's one or a series in a row. You'll find pendant lamps with open bottoms as well as those that are open on both bottom and top; the former sheds light only on the surface beneath it, while the latter illuminates above and below—like lamps with drum-style shades often found over dining tables.

Other good sources of general illumination are recessed lighting, in which downlights are placed evenly throughout a room, and track lighting, whereby you can position its movable fixtures to create a comfortable overall ambience. Both downlights and track lights should be evenly distributed. And both should be fitted with floodlights, which provide wide pools of light, rather than spotlights, which have concentrated beams. Finally, for a more architectural approach, consider cove lighting, installed on the wall behind a concave molding so that light shines upward and bounces off the ceiling. Because these three types all have a built-in nature, they benefit most from a well-thought-out lighting plan.

Ambient lighting has another important role, as it provides a support system for task and accent lighting; it's starting point, of sorts. Once a room's ambient lighting is in place, you can concentrate on illuminating specific surfaces and areas.

The high-style design of this room, coupled with a rich color palette, called for lighting fixtures that were simple but brilliant enough to illuminate the dark space. A four-arm chandelier shoulders much of the duty, providing general light while accenting the striped fabric on the ceiling, too.

above · While an elaborate chandelier is out of place in a kitchen, a smaller, less-formal style can add just the right touch of casual elegance. These twin fixtures are carefully spaced so they completely illuminate the island below.

left · Crystal lighting fixtures are no longer restricted to formal living quarters in high-end homes. They're more accessible and affordable than ever before, and are a good fit for any décor. This living room takes a style cue from the crystal chandelier, incorporating matching sconces on either side of the fireplace.

On the Right Track

There was a time when track lighting was little more than a straight stretch of metal interspersed with large can lights. Today, though, it's just as apt to curve its way around a room, with a variety of decorative lights suspended from the track by thin wires. You can even change the type of light along the way—from incandescent to high-intensity halogen and back again.

The track lighting in this living/dining area is, in fact, one of the elements that the spaces have in common, visually tying them together. Although their installations are different, exemplifying the versatility—one's straight as an arrow, the other encircles a skylight—the bulbs are similar, providing pinpoints of light in appropriate places.

above · During the day, this dining table is illuminated by the circular skylight above. At night, diners can appreciate the same effect, thanks to track lights that define the shape of the cutout.

left · In this living room, a stretch of track lighting is strategically positioned over an end wall where equidistantly placed bulbs showcase the art and accessories below. Against a dark backdrop, their beams take on an artistic quality that rivals the pieces they highlight.

Whatever type of ambient lighting you choose, don't feel that you're locked into a certain level of brightness. On the contrary, most rooms should have a certain amount of flexibility, depending upon the room's purpose and the mood you want to convey. It may sound like a tall order but, in fact, the solution is quite simple. Having more than one ambient source is one option. Or, by using dimmer switches—on one or more fixtures—you can change the lighting level at whim.

DIMMERS

One of the easiest and least expensive ways to add drama to a room, dimmers have long been used in the dining room. A festive family meal often calls for a brilliantly lit atmosphere, while a quiet dinner for two needs a more romantic ambiance. Today, though, dimmers can also be found in the kitchen, bedroom, bathroom, and anywhere else that can benefit from full-strength lighting but sometimes calls for a softer look. Be sure, however, that your fixture—and light source—is a good candidate for a dimmer switch. Check the back of the dimmer package to be sure, but, generally, fluorescent and halogen lights are not the best options nor are three-way switches. Dimmers come in toggle or dial styles and some are even touch-sensitive. Dimmer attachments are available, too, for floor and table lamps; on-line, socket, and plug-in dimmers can be found at home-improvement stores and lighting centers. Just be sure that the one you select is equipped to handle the total wattage of the light it controls.

left · **Drum-style shades were once reserved for table lamps, but today they're just as likely to be found on pendant fixtures, often in the kitchen or dining room because they spread such generous pools of light. This one provides both task and general lighting, and is supported by recessed lights around the ceiling's perimeter.**

Task Lighting

As its name implies, task lighting illuminates specific activities, whether it's cooking in the kitchen, reading in the study, or applying makeup in the master bath. In each case, the right lighting will make the job at hand easier. In living and bedroom areas, task lighting is often provided by table and floor lamps. Cone-shaped shades—with openings that are larger at the bottom than at the top—are good options for lamps, as they direct the majority of the light to the task at hand. If you select a shade that has similar-size openings at the top and bottom, it can serve double duty, illuminating the intended task and reflecting light off the ceiling, too. In some cases, you'll find that the inside of the shade differs in color from the outside; a crisp white shade, for instance, might have a pale pink interior, giving the light an even softer glow. Keep in mind, too, that lamps fitted with soft white bulbs—as opposed to those that are clear or colored—are easier on the eyes. To further control glare, use a three-way bulb or dimmer.

Downlights are an appropriate choice for task lighting in the kitchen. But this option is made even better when accompanied by lighting strips or puck lights positioned under wall cabinets and, perhaps, a pendant fixture or two over an island or sink. (To prevent working in the shadows, it's a good idea to use two or more fixtures to light the same surface from different directions.) In the bath, lights on either side of the mirror often work best; when positioned about 30 in. apart and at eye level, they illuminate the face evenly.

top · Gooseneck lamps are a popular choice for desktops because their light can be directed anywhere it's needed. Here, that concept has been translated to the bathroom, where delicate versions—lined up in a row—are positioned over the mirror.

bottom · This clean-lined, streamlined fixture—a stylish focal point in its own right—not only illuminates the dining table below but also bounces light back into the room.

Combining Kitchen Lighting Effectively

Task lighting is nowhere more important, perhaps, than in the kitchen. And in a well-designed room, it comes from more than one source. In this country kitchen, matching pendant lamps are spaced evenly, brightening the entire length of the island. There's plenty of light, whether you're prepping the meal or taking part in it. Because the pendants are translucent, they also boost the room's general lighting. Additionally, the glass shades, as well as the glass-fronted cabinets, bounce light—natural or otherwise—throughout the room.

Also taking on both general and task duties are the recessed lights around the room's perimeter. At full strength, they shed an abundance of light directly on the counters below, whether you're cooking at the stove or cleaning up at the sink. Even dimmed to a softer level, they can still help you find your way to the refrigerator for a midnight snack.

above · A pair of glass pendant lamps fulfill their primary purpose—task lighting—but also draw the eye toward the green-painted island, unquestionably the room's central focus.

left · Recessed lights are paramount to this kitchen, but natural light comes into play, too. Any amount of natural light is vital to a comfortable lighting plan.

There's more to adding a light to a room than simply setting it in place, particularly when it comes to task lighting. It's just as important that your lamp or fixture is positioned at the right height. Follow these guidelines:

• **Table and floor lamps**—Make sure that the shade of your table or floor lamp is neither too high nor too low. One with a shade that's too high will leave you staring at a bare bulb; one that's too low, on the other hand, will shed a pool of light on the table or floor but little else. Whether it's intended for task or ambient lighting, the bottom of a lamp's shade should be at eye level when someone is seated, approximately 38 in. to 42 in. from the floor.

• **Pendant lamps and chandeliers**—When using a pendant lamp or chandelier for task lighting purposes, it should be positioned so the bottom is approximately 30 in. above the surface that it illuminates, such as a dining table or a countertop. (To cut down on the glare of a bare bulb in a pendant fixture, especially over a dining table, consider replacing it with one that has a silver crown.) If the height of your room is more than 8 ft., though, raise the height of the fixture 2 in. to 3 in. per extra foot to create better visual balance. There's plenty of flexibility thanks to the adjustable chains and cords—even pulley systems—that these fixtures are suspended from.

above • When choosing a table lamp, think beyond its utilitarian purpose and take advantage of decorative possibilities, too. The base of this lamp is almost sculptural, putting it on equal footing with the other tabletop accessories.

facing page top • A floor lamp placed next to a chaise needs a certain amount of flexibility, as evidenced here. The light source will need to be higher if you're sitting up to read than if you're fully reclined.

facing page bottom • The lights over the vanity in this bathroom provide more than sufficient illumination. Plus, they carry out a subtle nautical theme, further enhanced by the overall blue-and-white scheme.

The Right Light

Today's light bulbs vary almost as much as the lighting fixtures they fit. In addition to assorted shapes and sizes, each bulb type gives off its own distinct glow. Here are the most common:

STANDARD INCANDESCENTS
$

- Inexpensive; readily available
- Relatively short-lived, typically less than 1,000 hours
- Provide good general lighting and are complementary to skin tones
- Work well with dimmers.

HALOGENS
$$

- Last between 2,250 and 3,500 hours
- More expensive than incandescent bulbs
- Generate considerable heat; can be a fire hazard
- Give off a clear, white light

FLUORESCENTS
$$

- Produce more light per watt than incandescents or halogens
- Can last more than 10,000 hours
- Compact fluorescents fit in standard light sockets
- Cast truer light than in the past; no more greenish tints

LOW-VOLTAGE LIGHTS
$$$

- With a built-in or remote transformer, most reduce 120-volt line current to 12 volts
- Fixtures cost approximately two to four times as much as their conventional counterparts, though they are less expensive to operate
- Bulbs last longer than standard incandescents

above · In a room with a subtle monochromatic theme, a variety of shape and texture is essential. This appealing mix is well thought out right down to the lighting, which includes wooden table lamps on either side of the bed and one with a metal base in front of the window.

facing page · This table lamp is anything but an afterthought. Its black drum shade provides a visual connecting point between a pair of black armchairs, giving the seating group a stronger presence in the process.

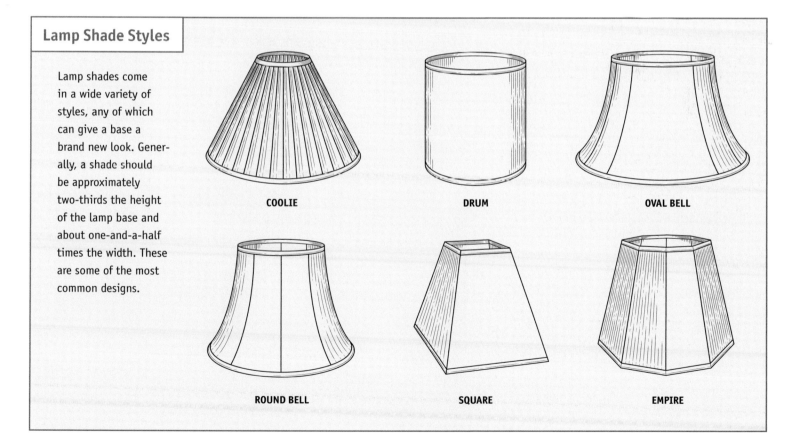

Lamp Shade Styles

Lamp shades come in a wide variety of styles, any of which can give a base a brand new look. Generally, a shade should be approximately two-thirds the height of the lamp base and about one-and-a-half times the width. These are some of the most common designs.

COOLIE

DRUM

OVAL BELL

ROUND BELL

SQUARE

EMPIRE

Accent Lighting

Accent lighting can be purely decorative or literally accent a particular piece of art. If you're looking for all-out drama, you might opt to wash a wall with light, perhaps to emphasize a decorative paint finish or a striking color. Position a light—or a whole row—on the ceiling; track or recessed fixtures, set approximately 2 ft. to 3 ft. from the wall (and angled in the same direction, if there's more than one) can beautifully bathe a wall in light. Likewise, a carefully placed uplight—a can-style fixture set on the floor—can cast light up onto a wall or even onto a houseplant such as a ficus tree or schefflera, making it look more spectacular.

If want to showcase something special, such as a work of art or architectural element, consider spotlights and track lights—their beams can be precisely aimed at any given object. Sconces and uplights can deliver, too, but no matter what type of light you use, be sure to follow this simple formula: Accent lighting, especially when used for true emphasis purposes, should be at least three times brighter than ambient lighting. That is, if the room's general light is provided by 50-watt bulbs, accent lighting should be at the 150-watt level.

Some accent lighting, too, can serve double duty. Wall sconces, for example, can generally illuminate a hallway and add a decorative aspect, too. (Be sure to mount sconces 5 ft. to 6 ft. off the floor; the higher the ceiling, the higher they should be hung.) Likewise, in the kitchen, a cable or rail system can light up an eating bar and provide visual interest at the same time.

facing page · The primary role of wall sconces in this family room is purely decorative. But because a work of art is positioned between them, it reaps the benefit of soft side lighting in addition to the glow it gets from recessed spots above.

left · Blue-tinted lighting at the base of each riser undoubtedly adds a decorative element to this staircase. But there's a practical purpose, as well: It can serve as a sophisticated night-light for anyone navigating the stairs in the dark.

below · For grooming in the bathroom, it's best to have light sources on either side of the vanity mirror. That same concept allows you to better see your reflection in a floor mirror, too. The sconces that flank this one also permit a last-minute, up-close inspection of makeup.

Lighting

No longer do you have to settle for a single overhead fixture in the center of the room. Today's vast options allow you to create various layers of light. With the right mix of ambient, task, and accent lighting, the same room can have many different moods—all it takes is a flip of the switch.

1. In this living room, general lighting provided by track lighting and a floor lamp takes a secondary role during the day, when natural light floods through the sliding glass doors. Recessed lights, meanwhile, brightly accent pieces of art at all hours. 2. In lieu of a single light source overhead, this trio of pendant lights serves the same purpose. This kind of fixture also allows you to bring the light source closer to the task at hand, particularly when ceilings are very high or cathedral style.

3. This pendant fixture casts a large pool of light on the dining table below. At the same time, however, it energizes the space with an unexpected splash—and source—of color. 4. Underscored by light, this chrome handrail—a good fit for contemporary settings like this—has a sculptural feeling. Plus, it offers an extra safety factor by shedding light squarely on the steps below. 5. In a room with a high ceiling, it's important to have visual interest at a variety of heights. This decorative pendant lamp does just that, softly lighting this corner in the process. Crystal beads spaced along the chains sparkle from the reflected light, making the fixture even more eye-catching.

FINISHING

A room isn't really complete until you've added decorative accessories, those

last few finishing touches that speak volumes about your personal style.

TOUCHES

But it's more than a mere fashion statement: Well-selected accessories

can make your friends feel welcome and your family "at home."

Accessorizing a Room

The furniture is in position. Your floor covering is fashionable, yet functional, and well-chosen lighting makes it all shine. So what's left? Decorative accessories. Accessorizing your home is no different than accessorizing an outfit—even haute couture needs the right finishing touches to complete the ensemble.

A well-accessorized room takes some forethought. If you have a piece of art that would be perfect over the fireplace, make it a part of your overall plan. With prominent placement, the artwork may become the focal point. Then, as you're selecting the rest of the room's furnishings, make sure they don't overwhelm—or detract from—the piece. Wall groupings of art or collectibles require a little preplanning, too, especially if you'll be devoting a considerable amount of space to the arrangement. Smaller groupings, such as framed photos or a collection of decorative boxes on a shelf—even a striking vase—can be added once everything else is in place.

But the right accessories will not only embellish a space but also play up your personality. They can speak of your travels, your tastes, and your heritage, making you feel more at home. Do your preferences run toward the traditional? If so, a collection of Wedgewood® plates may grace your dining room walls. But even contemporary, streamlined spaces need to be accessorized, even if only a single abstract painting. From time to time, rearrange things for a new perspective.

right • Assembling a mix of pillows on a seating piece is much like combining patterns throughout a room. Simply put together a large-scale print, a small- to medium-scale print, and a solid that all have at least one color in common.

Think outside the Box

Wall art isn't limited to paintings and prints. By thinking outside the box, you're bound to come up with any number of options. This collection of antique game boards, for instance, is right in step with the vintage chest below. Because one of the boards isn't hung directly on the wall but propped on top of the chest, the grouping blends seamlessly with a flock of carved birds, also of the same country genre.

above · With the right mix of elements, even the simplest tablescape can add dimension to a room. This vignette gets its visual interest from cream-colored components with a variety of textures—a lacey doily, a smooth ceramic bowl and pitcher, even the soft petals found in the floral arrangement.

left · Putting together a foursome is one of the easiest arrangements if all the artworks are the same size. Be sure to allow enough air between pieces to let them breathe but not so much that they appear as four singles instead of one cohesive whole.

Wall Art

Wall art, in its myriad forms, adds a personal touch to any room. It's the one element that should be chosen because it tugs at your heartstrings, not because it will fill a hole or match other furnishings in the room. (You've undoubtedly heard someone say that a particular piece "speaks" to him or her; there's more truth to that than you might think.)

Single, large works should always be given a place of prominence, perhaps over the fireplace or as a focal point at the end of a hall. Smaller pieces, on the other hand, have more flexibility. A single painting or print might be placed over a writing desk or in a powder room, where the small gem can be appreciated in its own right. Or you can give several small pieces more importance by making them part of a larger grouping. Even if they don't have similar subjects, you can create continuity by using the same mats and frames—you can't go wrong with something simple like cream-colored mats and black frames. Some other guidelines to keep in mind are:

• When positioning artwork over a sofa, the bottom of the piece should be about 8 in. higher than the back of the seating piece so people don't hit their heads on it.

• If a work of art is intended to be viewed by someone sitting in a chair, the center of the piece should be at eye level.

• Proper scale is important. Artwork over a sofa, for instance—whether it's a grouping or a single piece—should measure approximately two-thirds the length of the seating piece.

• Art arranged vertically will draw your eye up, making the room seem taller in the process. Conversely, horizontal arrangements can make a space seem wider than its actual dimensions.

above • Because this quartet of botanical prints is hung in close proximity to the lamps and other tabletop items below, the two areas visually become one, taking on more importance in the process. On either side of the arrangement, colorful robes seemingly frame the scheme.

below • The orange hue found in this contemporary work of art is echoed in a decorative plate on the nearby chest, visually connecting the two-dimensional art with the three-dimensional pieces below. A pair of topiaries prompt a double take; their simple forms make you rethink whether they're real or part of the artwork above.

Displaying Art and Collectibles

Composing wall groupings like these doesn't have to be difficult. Start with a piece of kraft paper (found at a local art-supply store) large enough to contain your finished grouping. Put it on the floor, and then arrange the elements you're using. Once you're satisfied, mark where the nail holes should be for each piece. Then, using painter's tape, attach the kraft paper to the wall. Drive nails or hangers into the appropriate places, then remove the paper from the wall. (If wall anchors are needed, determine their positions on the paper, but don't install them until after the paper's been removed.) Once all of the nails or hangers are in place, put each piece of art or collectible in its proper spot.

If you think that wall art consists of nothing more than paintings, posters, and prints, think again. Let your imagination run wild—you can hang practically anything that can be supported by a nail. From decorative plates to architectural elements—maybe a screen door or a piece of "gingerbread" from an old Victorian house—the possibilities are all but endless. Antique signs, a pair of snowshoes, even a shadow-boxed collection of matchboxes gathered during your travels can make eye-catching artworks. Consider decorative quilts and tapestries, too. A small one, the size of a crib quilt, for instance, can be framed in a conventional way, while something larger can be suspended from a decorative rod. Don't hesitate to use your own "artwork," either. With today's easy-to-use digital cameras and various ways to manipulate the size and color of your work, you can create your own "originals" with little time or money. Take an Andy Warhol approach, for example, and make four prints of a single image, each in a different monochromatic hue. Apply the images to stretched art canvases, and you have an art grouping that will make instant impact.

And what if your objects of art don't lend themselves to being hung on the wall? Many wall-hung shelf units can corral small items such as figurines and some are even works of art in their own right. To find one that suits your signature look, search in all of the usual places, but don't overlook flea markets, art fairs, and antiques stores.

top • Art groupings with common subjects and frames can create the effect of one large work. Additionally, the precisely lined-up pieces add an air of formality. Here, that tack is taken with two walls in close proximity, doubling the visual impact.

bottom • Take advantage of underused space such as a stairway wall. The placement of this dog-themed art allows people going up and down to see it up close. The arrangement works well because the bottom row of paintings is stair-stepped like the architecture itself.

Wall art doesn't need to be hung on the wall. This oversize piece is propped against the wall, although it's still secured in back to keep it from falling over. As a result, a room that could have looked very formal has a more laid back attitude.

Collectibles

Collectibles are, without a doubt, some of the most fun accessories to amass. They might include travel souvenirs, decorative bottles and boxes, even small treasures given to you by family and friends. But the bottom line is this: The more creative you are with what you consider a collectible, the more your room will speak of your personal style.

When considering possible groupings, start by placing all of the candidates on one large table. Put together combinations, keeping in mind that those with an odd number of objects are always more interesting than ones with an even number, particularly if you're working with just a few items. The eye tends to divide even-numbered groupings in half—and doesn't know which half to look at first. Varying heights is important, too; otherwise, one item tends to hide the next. If you're working with objects that have similar sizes and shapes, use small boxes and books as pedestals on which to set some of your collectibles. (When you come up with a combination that you particularly like, take a picture of it so you'll know how to reassemble it after cleaning day.) Remember, too, that decorative accessories in a given grouping need not be of the same vintage. In fact, it's much more interesting to mix old and new, fine objects with found items, hand-me-downs with newly purchased pieces. In some cases, try to incorporate an element of surprise as well—a small evergreen twig tucked among a collection of shiny glass, for instance. To find these unexpected elements, go shopping around your own home, keeping your eyes open indoors and out.

top · **Pieces of coral, in various sizes and shapes, form a fetching collection atop this chest. A propped-up mirror magnifies their importance, while a small lamp puts them in the proper spotlight.**

bottom · **Bookshelves can be utilized for more than your personal volumes. These are dedicated to accessories with a common theme —the beach. Prints of seaside landscapes and plenty of shells are artfully arranged, creating a mini-vacation for your mind's eye.**

above • With its upper doors thrown open wide, this painted armoire—a focal point in its own right—is even more eye-catching, thanks to the contents within. A collection of miniature chairs is compartmentalized, giving each example the attention it's due.

Displaying Collectibles

More than with any other accessory, the beauty of collectibles is truly in the eye of the beholder. Your preference may be fine porcelain or Pez® dispensers. You may have a few or what seems like a houseful. As long as your favorite collectible has meaning to you, it's an appropriate accent for your home.

1. Open shelves between two rooms allow you to fully appreciate fine collectibles, like these examples of art glass, from both vantage points. **2.** Collectibles need not be of the same exact type to be compatible. This collection of blue and white takes the form of plates, vases, and even a lamp—all perfectly at home with one another thanks to their common colors. **3.** A brilliant blue chest against a complementary orange wall provides the perfect backdrop of an equally colorful collection of pottery. **4.** The top of a chest or bureau can be much more than a convenient dropping-off spot—it can provide enough room for a colossal collection, like these miniature chairs. **5.** Something as practical as cowboy boots can add a personality-packed accent to a room, as long as it's artfully arranged.

Mantels

Accessorizing a mantel can seem mystifying unless you break it down to a few simple steps. First, determine how you want to approach the design. Does your room have a soaring cathedral ceiling? If so, your mantel—and the area above it—can handle a vertical arrangement. Or would you prefer to keep things more on eye level, creating a horizontal look that echoes the line of the mantel itself? Beyond that, mantel arrangements typically fall into one of two categories: those with formal, symmetrical balance and those with a more informal, asymmetrical style.

SYMMETRICAL BALANCE

Symmetrical balance is similar to mirror imagery. If you were to divide the wall above your mantel in half, each portion would be decorated exactly the same way. Typically used in traditional settings, symmetrical arrangements most often rely on objects that are identical. It's not a requirement, though, as long as the objects on each side are similar enough to create the sense of a perfect match. While symmetrical balance is easy to attain, it does have one drawback: If your items don't have enough visual excitement, the look runs the risk of becoming boring.

ASYMMETRICAL BALANCE

Groupings characterized by an even distribution of size, or visual "weight," fall into the asymmetrical balance category. For example, you might have a set of three candlesticks (in varying heights) on one side of the mantel and a tall rectangular box (for fireplace matches) on the other. They're entirely different elements, but they carry the same visual weight. Asymmetrical arrangements are also likely to incorporate large and small items, short and tall, all the way across the mantel—leaving just a few open spots here and there to allow for breathing room.

above · The only thing not perfectly symmetrical about this mantel arrangement is the architectural baluster. Because its design differs slightly from one end to the other, it adds just the slightest casual air to this otherwise formal configuration.

above · Why settle for a conventional work of art when you can use something that's one-of-a-kind? This cross section of wood has been carved into a stunning sculpture. Because it's set against a subtle, cream-colored backdrop, it becomes even more prominent.

A three-dimensional version of a sailing ship takes center stage over this stone fireplace. Directly beneath the artwork, decorative dishes with the same nautical theme visually connect the large piece to the mantel below.

Mantel Arrangements

Mantel arrangements run the gamut from utilizing a single painting to covering the entire surface—front to back and end to end. The important thing is that the display reflects the mood of the room. A contemporary space, with minimal furnishings, is a good candidate for something understated, while cottage-style decorating calls for more of a layered look.

1. There's no hard-and-fast rule that says a mantel has to be directly over the fireplace. The placement of this one gives it more prominence, as does the apple green color. 2. The size and shape of these three framed photographs create a sense of rhythm, echoing the paneled architecture directly in back of them. Pure white vases interspersed between the artworks give a greater sense of dimension. 3. Although not perfectly matched from side to side, this mantel arrangement appears so; the unlike items on either side of the mirror are similar in size, so they carry the same visual weight. 4. This asymmetrical arrangement works well because one of the mantel-top elements reaches higher than the bottom of the painting, bringing the beach-themed collectibles and artwork together as a cohesive whole. 5. Symmetrical mantel arrangements are most at home in formal settings. The tall candlesticks and Staffordshire dogs that grace this mantel, for instance, are just as traditional as the rest of the room.

Soft Stuff

When it comes to making a house a home, it's just not complete without a few soft touches. An accent pillow here, a cozy throw there . . . they all add up to a sense of warmth. What's more, these kinds of accessories are both fashionable and functional.

There's a wide range of decorative pillows available today in every imaginable style—needlepoint versions for the traditionalist, hand-hooked varieties for country enthusiasts, and colorful, graphic forms for contemporary fans. When displaying your favorite pillows, take the same approach as you would with any other collectible: Group together several similar ones to make a dramatic impact. To plump up a sofa, use two matching pillows (one at each end), then couple them with two slightly smaller versions that are complementary but not precisely the same size, shape, or pattern. Finally, place a rectangular lumbar pillow at the center of the seating piece, preferably something that makes a personal statement, like one with a monogram.

Throws, in soft yarns such as chenille and cashmere, are equally appealing to the eye and the psyche; draped over the arm of the chair, they not only can add a splash of color but also are always ready to wrap up in. Bed linens, too, have come a long way. No longer dressed with simple bedspreads and pillowcases, today's sleeping spots have multiple layers of linens that warrant closets of their own. Try to resist the temptation, though, to match everything perfectly; mixing and matching always results in a more appealing look.

In the case of handmade quilts, admire them for the works of art that they are in addition to—or instead of—using them for their more practical purpose. Hang one over your bed in lieu of a conventional headboard or drape a couple of them over the open doors of an armoire. Show just as much creativity as the stitched piece itself.

above • Decorative boudoir and neckroll pillows give a luxurious look to this bed, but it's the gauzy bed curtains that add real romance. And the curtains are just as practical as they are pretty. They allow light from the bedside lamp to shine through, making reading in bed possible.

above • Inspired by the predominant color of the quilt, a blue-and-white fabric with a calligraphy pattern takes a variety of forms. Not only does it show up on the different styles of pillows, making the window seat even more comfy, but it's also repeated on the nearby ottoman, creating design continuity.

Bed linens and quilts add a soft touch to this sleeping spot, executed in a simple red-and-white color scheme. Patterns and prints show up in a variety of small-to-large scales, but the two common colors hold the look together.

right • A soft tone-on-tone scheme is a restful choice for any bedroom. The right amount of texture, however—exemplified in this mix of linens—keeps it from becoming a snooze.

below • A whimsical rug was the inspiration for this colorful collection of pillows. Had the pillows each sported a pattern, the profusion could have become overwhelming; the solid colors balance the look beautifully.

Building on the Basics

A smart approach to decorating is to start with the basics, then build with accessories, as proven by this casual living space. Furnishings are, for the most part, white, with just a splash of blue here and there; the real color and pattern comes from the accessories. Decorative pillows, all in crisp blues and greens, provide layers of visual interest via their different patterns. Even a green throw gets into the act, breaking up the chaise's solid blue slipcover.

The real beauty of this décor lies in the fact that the pillows and throw can be changed out at a moment's notice, potentially creating a vastly different color scheme. Even the slipcover is an example of quick-change artistry in action. It can be switched seasonally or removed entirely to reveal the underlying upholstery.

above • In a colorful scheme, a touch of white can be a welcome resting place for the eye. Here, just the opposite is true—a blue slipcovered chaise offers visual relief in this predominantly white room.

This room's predominant blue hue is repeated in the rings that join the upper and lower curtain panels, serving as another accessory of sorts.

CREDITS

p. i: © Jessie Walker

p. ii: © Tria Giovan

p. iv: Left to right: © Eric Roth; © Eric Roth; © davidduncanlivingston.com; © davidduncanlivingston.com; © Eric Roth

p. v: Left to right: © davidduncanlivingston.com; © Mark Lohman; © Eric Roth; © Eric Roth; © Brian Vanden Brink, Photographer 2006

p. vii: © davidduncanlivingston.com

p. 1: © Tria Giovan

p. 3: Top left to right: © davidduncanlivingston.com; © Mark Lohman; © Eric Roth; © Brian Vanden Brink, Photographer 2006; © Eric Roth; bottom: © davidduncanlivingston.com

p. 4: © Eric Roth

Chapter 1

p. 4: © Tria Giovan; design: Mary Evelyn McKee

p. 6: Top and bottom: © Eric Roth; design: Americana Designs

p. 8: Top: © Jessie Walker; bottom: © Brian Vanden Brink, Photographer 2006; design: Green Company Architects

p. 9: © Tim Street-Porter; design: Annie Kelly

p. 10: © Jessie Walker

p. 11: Top: © Eric Roth; design: Glod Restoration & Renovation; bottom: © Tim Street-Porter; design: Annie Kelly

p. 12: © davidduncanlivingston.com

p. 13: Top: © davidduncanlivingston.com; bottom: © Tria Giovan

pp. 14–15: © Eric Roth; design: Stirling Brown Architects

p. 16: Top: © davidduncanlivingston.com; bottom: © Tria Giovan

p. 17: © Eric Roth

pp. 18–19: © Mark Lohman; design: Douglas Burdge Architects

pp. 20–23: © davidduncanlivingston.com

p. 24: Top: © Mark Lohman; design: Douglas Burdge Architects; bottom; © davidduncanlivingston.com

p. 25: © Tria Giovan; design: Renea Abbott

pp. 26–27: © Eric Roth; design: Niemitz Design

Chapter 2

p. 28: © davidduncanlivingston.com

p. 30: © davidduncanlivingston.com

p. 31: Top left: © davidduncanlivingston.com; top right: © Tria Giovan; bottom: © Tim Street-Porter; design: Tucker & Marks

p. 32: Top: © Mark Lohman; design: Janet Lohman Design; bottom: © davidduncanlivingston.com

p. 33: © Mark Lohman; design: Kyser Interiors

p. 34: © davidduncanlivingston.com

p. 35: Top: © Eric Roth; bottom: © Tria Giovan; design: Robin Bell

p. 36: Top: © Ken Gutmaker; bottom: © Eric Roth; design: Susan Sargent Designs

p. 37: © davidduncanlivingston.com

p. 38: Top: © Ken Gutmaker; bottom: © Tim Street-Porter; design: Tucker & Marks

p. 39: © Mark Lohman; design: Barclay Butera, Inc.

p. 40: © Eric Roth; design: Susan Sargent Designs

p. 41: Top: © Eric Roth; bottom left: © Ken Gutmaker; bottom right: © Jessie Walker; design: Colette McKerr

p. 42: © Eric Roth; design: Frank Roop Design + Interiors

p. 43: © Eric Roth

p. 44: © Mark Lohman; design: Janet Lohman Interior Design

p. 45: Top: © Ken Gutmaker; bottom left: © Mark Lohman; design: Janet Lohman Interior Design; bottom right: © davidduncanlivingston.com

p. 46: Top: © Mark Lohman; design: Janet Lohman Interior Design; bottom: © Steve Vierra; design: Diana Bell

p. 47: © Mark Lohman; design: Susan Cohen Interior Design

p. 48: © Mark Lohman; design: Janet Lohman Interior Design

p. 49: © Tim Street-Porter; design: Martyn Lawrence Bullard

p. 50: Top: © Mark Lohman; design: Janet Lohman Interior Design; bottom: © davidduncanlivingston.com

p. 51: © Mark Lohman; design: Barclay Butera , Inc.

p. 52: © davidduncanlivingston.com

p. 53: © Eric Roth; design: Susan Sargent Designs

p. 54: Top left: © Eric Roth; design: Trikeenan Tile Works; top right: © Mark Lohman; design: William Hefner Architects; bottom right: © Steve Vierra; design: Decorative Interiors

p. 55: © Mark Lohman; design: Bianchi Design

pp. 56–57: © Eric Roth; design: Benjamin Nutter Associates, Architects

Chapter 3

p. 58: © davidduncanlivingston.com

p. 60: Top: © davidduncanlivingston.com; bottom: © Mark Samu, Samu Studios, Inc.; design: Lucianna Samu Design

p. 61: © davidduncanlivingston.com

p. 62: © Ken Gutmaker

p. 63: © Eric Roth; design: Frank Roop Design + Interiors

p. 64: Top: © Brian Vanden Brink, Photographer 2006; bottom: © davidduncanlivingston.com

p. 65: Top left: © Mark Lohman; design: Douglas Burdge Architects; right and bottom left: © davidduncanlivingston.com

p. 66: Top: © Mark Lohman; design: Janet Lohman Interior Design; bottom: © Steve Vierra; design: Marian Glasglow

p. 67: © Mark Lohman; design: Barclay Butera, Inc.

p. 68: Left: © Eric Roth; design: Benjamin Nutter Associates, Architects; right: © davidduncanlivingston.com

p. 69: Left: © Brian Vanden Brink, Photographer 2006; right: © Eric Roth; design: Trikeenan Tileworks

p. 70: Top: © davidduncanlivingston. com; bottom: © Randy O'Rourke

p. 71: © Tim Street-Porter; design: Jean-Luis Deniot

p. 72: Top: © davidduncanlivingston.com; bottom: courtesy Ann Sacks/The Kohler Co.

p. 73: Left: © Tim Street-Porter; design: Jean-Luis Deniot; top right and bottom right: courtesy Ann Sacks/ The Kohler Co.

p. 74: Top: © Eric Roth; design: Trikeenan Tileworks; bottom: © Eric Roth; design: Thomas Buckborough & Associates

p. 75: Top: Eric Roth; design: Stern McCafferty; bottom: © Eric Roth; design: Trikeenan Tile Works

p. 76: Left: © Ken Gutmaker; top right: © Jessie Walker; design: Gail Drury, CKD, CBD, Drury Design; bottom right: © davidduncanlivingston.com

p. 77: Top left: © Carolyn Bates; design: Milford Cushman, The Cushman Design Group; general contractor; Patterson & Smith Construction; top right and bottom left: © davidduncanlivingston.com

p. 158: © davidduncanlivingston.com

p. 159: Top: © davidduncanlivingston. com; bottom: © Brian Vanden Brink, Photographer 2006; design: John Morris Architects

p. 160: © Eric Roth

p. 161: Top and bottom: © Eric Roth; bottom design: Manual de Santaren, Inc.

p. 162: Top right: © Eric Roth; design: www.wolferslighting.com; bottom left: © Eric Roth; design: Susan Sargent Designs; bottom right: © Brian Vanden Brink, Photographer 2006; design: Quinn Evans Architects

p. 163: Top: © Eric Roth; design: Gleysteen Architects; bottom: © Alise O'Brien; design: Colleen Horner Kitchen, Bath, Tile, and Stone

p. 164: © davidduncanlivingston.com

p. 165: © Mark Lohman; design: Douglas Burdge Architects

p. 166: Left: © Brian Vanden Brink, Photographer 2006; top: © Eric Roth; design: K Marshall Design; bottom right: © Eric Roth; design: Molly Skok Design

p. 167: Top: © Eric Roth; design: Sheer & White Architects; bottom: © Eric Roth; design: Horst Buchanan Architects

p. 168: Top: © davidduncanlivingston. com; bottom: © Jessie Walker; design: Meegan McMillan

p. 169: © davidduncanlivingston.com

p. 170: © Mark Lohman; design: Douglas Burdge Architects

p. 171: Top: © davidduncanlivingston. com; bottom: © Brian Vanden Brink, Photographer 2006

p. 172: © davidduncanlivingston.com

p. 173: Top left: © Tim Street-Porter; top right: © Mark Samu, Samu Studios, Inc.; design: Riverside Furniture bottom: © Eric Roth; design: Americana Designs

p. 174: © davidduncanlivingston.com

p. 175: Top: © Mark Lohman: design; Janet Lohman Interior Design; bottom left: © Eric Roth; design: Manual de Santaren, Inc. bottom right: © davidduncanlivingston.com

p. 176: © Brian Vanden Brink, Photographer 2006

p. 177: Left: © Chipper Hatter; design: Bill McMillin Interiors; right: © davidduncanlivingston.com

p. 178: © Eric Roth; design: Sheer & White Architects

p. 179: Top: © davidduncanlivingston. com; bottom: © Eric Roth

p. 180: © davidduncanlivingston.com

p. 181: © davidduncanlivingston.com

p. 182: © Eric Roth; design: Details

p. 183: © Eric Roth; design: Frank Roop Design + Interiors

p. 184: © Brian Vanden Brink, Photographer 2006; design: Green Company Architects

p. 185: Top: © Brian Vanden Brink, Photographer 2006; bottom left: © Tim Street-Porter; design: Annie Kelly; bottom right: © Rob Karosis; design: Vetter Dink Architects

p. 186: © Eric Roth; design: Frank Roop Design + Interiors

p. 187: Top left: © Brian Vanden Brink, Photographer 2006; top right: © davidduncanlivingston.com; bottom: © Mark Lohman

p. 188: Top: © davidduncanlivingston. com; bottom: © Eric Roth; design: Catalano Architects

p. 189: Right: © Brian Vanden Brink, Photographer 2006; design: Susan Thorn Interior Design; left: © Ken Gutmaker

p. 190: Left and top right: © davidduncanlivingston.com; bottom right: © Eric Roth; design: Stirling Brown Architects

p. 191: © Brian Vanden Brink, Photographer 2006

pp. 192–193: © Mark Samu, Samu Studios, Inc.; design; Lucianna Samu Designs

p. 194: © davidduncanlivingston.com

p. 195: Top: © Mark Lohman; design: Kyser Interiors; bottom: © Tim Street-Porter

Chapter 6

p. 196: © Tria Giovan

p. 198: © davidduncanlivingston.com

p. 199: © Eric Roth; design: Terrat Elms Design

p. 200: © Eric Roth

p. 201: © davidduncanlivingston.com

pp. 202–203: © Eric Roth; design: Stern McCafferty

p. 204: © davidduncanlivingston.com

p. 205: Top: © Eric Roth; bottom: © davidduncanlivingston.com

p. 206: © davidduncanlivingston.com

p. 207: Top left: © Tria Giovan; top right: © Mark Lohman; design: Barclay Butera, Inc. bottom left: © davidduncanlivingston.com; bottom right: © Tim Street-Porter; design: Thomas Callaway

p. 208: Top: © Jessie Walker Associates; design: Meegan McMillan; bottom: © Eric Roth

p. 209: © Eric Roth; design: Americana Designs

p. 210: Top: © Steve Vierra; design: Shelley Weiss; bottom: © davidduncanlivingston.com

p. 211: © Steve Vierra; design: Pamela Baker

p. 212: © Brian Vanden Brink, Photographer 2006; design: Whitten & Winkelman Architects

p. 213: Top left and bottom left: © davidduncanlivingston.com; right: © Brian Vanden Brink, Photographer 2006

p. 214: © Mark Lohman; design: Barclay Butera, Inc.

p. 215: Top: © davidduncanlivingston. com; bottom: © Eric Roth; design: Americana Designs

p. 216: Left: © davidduncanlivingston.com; right: © Brian Vanden Brink, Photographer 2006; design: John Colomarino, Architect

p. 217: © Mark Samu, Samu Studios, Inc.; design: Donalds Billinkoff Architect

p. 218: Left: © Brian Vanden Brink, Photographer 2006; right: © Rob Karosis; design: Doug Cogger, The Great Room Company

p. 219: Top: © Eric Roth; design: Bill Powell; bottom: © davidduncanlivingston.com

p. 220: Top: © davidduncanlivingston.com; bottom: © Brian Vanden Brink, Photographer 2006

p. 221: © davidduncanlivingston.com

p. 222: Top: © davidduncanlivingston.com; bottom: © Ken Gutmaker

p. 223: © Steve Vierra; design: Maniseh Emery

p. 224: Left: © Rob Karosis; design: Dwight McNeil Architects; right: © davidduncanlivingston.com

p. 225: courtesy Canac/Kohler Co.

p. 226: © Brian Vanden Brink, Photographer 2006

p. 227: Top: © Mark Samu, Samu Studios, Inc.; design: Donald Billinkoff Architect; bottom left: © Tria Giovan; bottom right: © Ken Gutmaker

p. 228: Top: © Eric Roth; design: Sheer & White Architects; bottom: © Tria Giovan; design: Mary Evelyn McKee

p. 229: © Rob Karosis; design: Richard Williams, Architect

p. 230: Top: © Eric Roth; bottom: © davidduncanlivingston.com

INDEX

MORE GREAT IDEAS THAT REALLY WORK

KITCHEN IDEAS THAT WORK

Beth Veillette
Paperback
ISBN 13: 978-156158-837-4
ISBN10: 1-56158-837-7
EAN: 9781561588374
9 x 10½
240 pages
382 full color photographs
   throughout
27 drawings
Product # 070883
$19.95 U.S., $25.95 Can.
Available

DECORATING IDEAS THAT WORK

Heather J. Paper
Paperback
ISBN 13: 978-156158-950-0
ISBN10: 1-56158-950-0
EAN: 9781561589500
9 x 10½
288 pages
475 full color photographs
   throughout
30 drawings
Product # 070962
$21.95 U.S., $27.95 Can.
Available October 2007

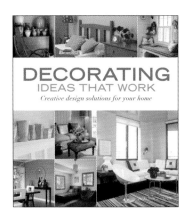

BATHROOM IDEAS THAT WORK

Scott Gibson
Paperback
ISBN 13: 978-156158-836-7
ISBN10: 1-56158-836-9
EAN: 9781561588367
9 x 10½
224 pages
367 full color photographs
   throughout
17 drawings
Product # 070884
$19.95 U.S., $25.95 Can.
Available

OUTDOOR KITCHEN IDEAS THAT WORK

Lee Anne White
Paperback
ISBN 13: 978-156158-958-6
ISBN10: 1-56158-958-6
EAN: 9781561589586
9 x 10½
224 pages
350 full color photographs
   throughout
30 drawings
Product # 070968
$19.95 U.S., $25.95 Can.
Available January 2008

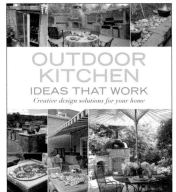